CHINA IN THE 21ST CENTURY SERIES

CHINA: HAS THE LAST OPPORTUNITY PASSED BY?!

CHINA IN THE 21ST CENTURY SERIES

China in World Affairs
V. Clarence (Editor)
ISBN 1-56072-359-9

Crisis and Reform in China
E. Bliney
ISBN 1-56072-416-1

China's Relations with Japan in an Era...
Dong Dong Zhang (Editor)
ISBN 1-56072-625-3

Bicoastal China: A Dialectical, Paradigmatic Analysis
Peter Kien-hong Yu
ISBN 1-56072-640-7

The Political Dynamics of Hong Kong Under the Chinese Sovereignty
Jermain T.M. Lam
ISBN 1-56072-806-X

US China Policy: Interest Groups and Their Influence
H. Comet
2001. ISBN 1-59033-044-7

China: Possible Missile Technology Transfers
Shirley A. Kan (Editor)
2003. ISBN 1-59033-758-1

FDI in China: Contributions to Growth, Restructuring and Competitiveness
Jiang Xiaojuan
2003. ISBN 1-59033-894-4

Government and Market in China: A Local Perspective
Jian Zhang (Editor)
2004. ISBN 1-59033-883-9

China's Telecommunications Reforms: From Monopoly towards Competition
Scott Yunxiang Guan
2007. ISBN 1-59033-540-6

China and Antiterrorism
Simon Shen (Editor)
2007. ISBN 1-60021-344-8

China-U.S. Economic and Geopolitical Relations
Jerald D. Finn (Editor)
2008. ISBN 978-1-60456-052-7

Education in China
James U. Landowe (Editor)
2008. ISBN 978-1-60456-309-2

Trade Barriers and China
Martha B. Kessler
2008. ISBN 978-1-60456-686-4

China Naval Modernization: Implications for U.S. Navy Capabilities
Ronald O'Rourke
2008. ISBN 978-1-60456-709-0

Is China A Threat to the U.S. Economy?
Craig K. Elwell, Marc Labonte and Wayne M. Morrison
2008. ISBN 978-1-60456-843-1

Congress and US China Policy
Jian Yang (Editor)
2008. ISBN 1-56072-844-2

Human Rights in China
Lee R. Massingdale (Editor)
2009. ISBN 978-1-60741-116-1

China: Has the Last Opportunity Passed By?!
Guang Wu
2009. ISBN 978-1-60741-538-1

CHINA IN THE 21ST CENTURY SERIES

CHINA: HAS THE LAST OPPORTUNITY PASSED BY?!

GUANG WU

Nova Science Publishers, Inc.
New York

For permission to use material from this book please contact us:
Telephone 631-231-7269; Fax 631-231-8175
Web Site: http://www.novapublishers.com

LIBRARY OF CONGRESS CATALOGING-IN-PUBLICATION DATA

Wu, Guang.
China : has the last opportunity passed by?! / Guang Wu.
p. cm.
Includes bibliographical references and index.
ISBN 978-1-60741-538-1 (hardcover : alk. paper)
1. China--Politics and government--2002- 2. China--Economic conditions--2000- 3. China--Civilization. I. Title.
DS779.46.W8 009
951.06--dc22 2009010503

Published by Nova Science Publishers, Inc. † New York

Dedicated to my Beloved Parents,
Qinghe Wu and Heqing Zhou

Contents

PREFACE

The Historically Unique Opportunity. The first couple of years at the beginning of 21st century were the historically unique opportunity for China, not only because the Chinese economy grew amazingly, which shocked the world, but also more importantly the US was busy in the war on terror, and Russia was still not recovered from the collapse of Soviet Union and was undergoing a painfully chaotic phase in her modern history.

When looking at other world powers at that moment, Japan was in deep trouble with her economy, the reunion overwhelmed Germany with her extremely high unemployment rate, even all the Europe were paralyzed although the UK was immune from the difficulty in European continent.

When looking back Chinese history, China as a nation never had such a powerful time equipped with modern technology and knowledge although there were several great episodes in Chinese history, the Chinese then had no means to go beyond their border.

In 2008, the history was slowly changing to another direction, the war on terror, though difficult, is approaching to stable if not the end, and there is no any major attack on the US soil, the new Russia is getting up, Germany is going out from her bottom, Japan is stable and creeping from her bottom, India appears in global screen, although the world is going to recession. Certainly the Chinese economy will continue growing, but the window of opportunity, through which China can become a world power, has gone.

This is the unique opportunity for Chinese people over her 5000-plus-year history, in this book I will explore why the Chinese had lost this opportunity.

The Oldest Theme. In 1987, I studied as an MS student in Beijing, China. During an English examination, I noticed our professor, who was monitoring our written examination, was busy reading a book, which is entitled "The Ugly

Chinaman" [1]. That was the first time for me to know this book, although I had no time to read it at that time. It was then the time that the Chinese people were thinking the way, by which China could become stronger, and people frequently discussed the topic of why China is underdeveloped. From 1988 to 1992, I was a state-commissioned PhD student in Ukraine, USSR, then Russia, the hottest topic discussed among Chinese students was why China lagged behind the world, in fact lagged behind the industrialized world, over last one or two hundred years. Of course, these hot discussions generally ended up without any definite answers, besides leaving us puzzled.

From 1992 to 2002, I did my postdoc in Italy, Japan, Italy, France and then worked in Switzerland, but this theme never came to my mind. Perhaps, this topic also escaped from notice of Chinese people because the Chinese economy grew really fast, thanks to the great reform initiated by Deng Xiaoping.

However, one day when I accompanied my son going to his school, then it was 2004 and I lived in Yiantian, Shenzhen, Province Guangdong, China, he asked me why China with her 5000-plus year civilization lagged behind the industrialized world over the last one or two hundred years, I told him that there is no answer to this question, which has been intensively discussed over many years in uncountable occasions.

Possible Answer to Another Question. From 2007 to 2008, I lived in Yangshuo, Province Guangxi, China for writing the book, Lecture Notes on Computational Mutation [2], after finished it, the extremely beautiful landscape of Yangshuo made me recall the oldest theme of why China lagged behind the industrialized world for the last one or two hundred years. The book, The Ugly Chinaman [1], once again reappeared from my memory, I found it, and gave a glance at it. Thereafter I began to consider this theme seriously for the first time. However, I should admit that I did not spend too much time in considering this theme, though seriously, because I am more interested in a relevant topic, which is the natural consequence of this topic. That is, I am more interested in the topics of how China can become a world power as many Chinese dream for generations, and why China has lost her historically unique opportunity, which I defined. In summer 2008, I lived in Nanning, Province Guangxi, China, where I frequently met an Englishman, who taught the English in University of Guangxi, in swimming pool. We sometimes discussed the possible outcome for the incoming Olympic game in Beijing, and about China, then I told him my view that China has lost her historically unique opportunity, which surprised him a lot, because he thought that there would be a great opportunity waiting for China in future, which is a quite popular view in many people. Likely I need to write down my argument, this book is the reflection of my meditations.

For this small book, I did not ask the Publishers for English editing, because this small book represents my real level of English, I do not pretend to be great in English, which would not be me. Please accept my deepest apology for the difficulty in reading of this small book.

Guang Wu
February 10, 2009
China

Chapter 1

HISTORICALLY UNIQUE OPPORTUNITY

The world in first couple of years in 21st century offered many opportunities, although this period of time is one of longest peaceful and prosperous times in human history.

First, the world order and structure established based on the direct results of World War II completely do not exist anymore, because of the collapse of Soviet Union and her satellite states. This means that almost all the international organizations are in a questionable position, because their aims were designed based on the order and structure established immediately after World War II.

Second, no major systematical theories appear on how to fairly distribute the social wealth and how to fairly exercise the social justice since Marxism and Leninism. Although the capitalism did well when competing with socialism and communism over the last one hundred years, it would, by common sense, be stall without real competition with other social systems such as socialism and communism as evidenced that the capitalism well developed in the US but did not function well in Western Europe and Japan for that period. Moreover, a single capitalism could not fill the vacuum fully, because the mankind needs diversity, thus various thoughts reappear and become fashionable, such as consumerism, Islam, etc.

Third, there are no solutions for many old problems, which exist since World War II, for example, Arab-Israeli conflict, North-South conversation, poverty, etc., but new problems appear more than before, for instance, global warming, city congestion, etc.

Fourth, many international treaties appear to be out-of-date, for example, the Nuclear Non-Proliferation Treaty, North Atlantic Treaty Organization, etc.

Fifth, the working class is vanishing and trade union is dying worldwide. This means that there will soon be no dominant class in any modern social systems, which should be a new phenomenon in human history.

Likely, any country with solution to any of these challenges would relatively easily become a world leader or hold an important position in this new world. For example, the Leninism provides a solution for Russia, which could not win the Russo-Japanese War in 1904-1905 and the World War I in 1917. Similarly the Maoism provides a solution for China, which suffered the consistent chaos and humilities for almost one or two hundred years.

This opportunity is also possible not only because the Americans were still happy with their super position in the world without thinking of solutions, but also because the Americans were busy in the war on terror.

In short, this period of time was a historically unique opportunity not only for the US, which peaked in 2000, but also for China that was then rapidly approaching to her historical peak. This is so because these two countries were not involved in painful and dramatic transforms during the 90s of 20th century. In this sense, the economic reform designed by Dong Xiaoping is much less painful than the reforms in former Soviet bloc.

The absolute level of peak reached by the Chinese was not as high as the peaks reached by Americans, French, Japanese, German, Russian and British in modern history, however the relative level was higher than others at that period because these world powers were in deep trouble as Japan was in trouble with her economy, Germany suffered from her reunion with extremely high unemployment rate, even the whole Europe were paralyzed although the UK was immune from the difficulty in European continent. Moreover, the speed of China approaching her peak was amazingly fast, which, unlike the speed once was in Soviet Union, is widely reported. This impact is not comparable.

Yet, another important advantage for Chinese is that China was not bound to many international treaties and obligations then.

This is a very short window of opportunity for China, because the common logic and sense tell us the only path after reaching the peak is to go down if not stable. During that period of time, China was rapidly approaching her peak with her 20-plus-year reforms, but meanwhile other world powers were going down from their peaks.

In Chinese history, there were perhaps several similar opportunities appeared in front of Chinese people. China would have become a regional leader at least if the Chinese would have taken the advantage from these opportunities.

The first opportunity would be the time when the Emperor Qin Shihuang (259 BC –210 BC) unified China in 221 BC, he has a very strong army with very experienced generals and soldiers in real combats in unifying of China. In fact, it would be the time for China to expend her influence, even her territory into the Central Asia. However, Emperor Qin Shihuang destroyed the weapons captured from defeated kingdoms, and began his plan to build the Great Wall to defend non-Chinese although his troops had already reach the Central Asia [3]. Arguably the building of Great Wall marks the beginning of decline of dynasty Qin. If we look at the means, which the Chinese had during this first opportunity, then it was the very experienced and powerful army. Otherwise, the Chinese history on that period of time should be fabricated if this opportunity is not the case.

The second opportunity would be the time of dynasty Tang (618 AD - 907 AD), then the culture and industry were well developed, and the best time for the well-known Silk Road. But the potential advantage for this opportunity would be smaller than the first one, because foreign nationals were likely much stronger than the time of dynasty Qin. Therefore, Emperor Li Shimin (599 AD – 649 AD) was busy sending his so-called daughters to neighboring countries to marry their kings in order to fix the relationship between countries with marriage as done by European powers in history. The famous example would be the princess Wencheng, who married Songtsän Gampo [4]. If we look at the means, which the Chinese had during this second opportunity, then it was the superior Chinese civilization. Otherwise, the Chinese civilization should be below other civilizations if this opportunity is not the case.

The third opportunity would be the time of finishing World War II, then China as a victory country could easily obtain some priority not limited to a position in UN Security Council. Of course, China was much weaker during this opportunity than in previous two opportunities. The only means, which the Chinese had during this third opportunity, was to ask a certain amount of reparations from Japan. Otherwise, the surrender of Japan should not be unconditioned if this opportunity is not the case.

Based on the circumstances mentioned above, more than certain, the first couple of years in 21st century are the fourth opportunity for the Chinese, arguably the best and historically unique opportunity for Chinese over their history and in foreseeing years, not only because China as a nation never had such a powerful time equipped with modern technology and knowledge, but also the long-term trend during Chinese 5000-plus-year history suggests that China progressively becomes weaker and weaker during the first three opportunities, thus the fourth opportunity could be a spike or a turning point during Chinese history.

However, this best and historically unique opportunity passed silently without notice and pity. The world has changed dramatically since 2008: the war on terror, though difficult, is approaching to stable if not the end because there is no any major attack on the US soil, the new Russia is getting up, Germany is going out from her bottom, Japan is stable and creeping from her bottom, India appears in global screen. Although the entire world is going to recession, China cannot be immune.

In fact, the collapse of price of crude oil, which peaked around the opening of Olympic Game in Beijing in 2008, is very suggestive from the internationally political viewpoint, say, the focus of international politics shifted from China to Russia, Iran, and Venezuela, because the high price is no good for China, but good for Russia, Iran, and Venezuela, while the low price is no good for Russia, Iran, and Venezuela, but good for China. China is no longer the threat to the world and is no longer important, thus she can enjoy the oil with low price. This is very similar to the fact that currently no one blames Japan for possibly manipulating her currency, because Japan as a nation is no longer significant in current world.

Chance favors only those who know how to court her [5]. It is very clear that we, Chinese, did not see these four opportunities since the birth of our national and therefore could not seize these opportunities. Actually neither Chinese nor non-Chinese noticed these four opportunities for Chinese, while the fourth would arguably be the last opportunity for Chinese?

If the October revolution in 1917 in Russia would be a direct result from the analysis far before the revolution 1905 [6], the lost of this opportunity would be a direct result from Chinese themselves, their characteristics, their thoughts, and their traditions.

Chapter 2

WHAT MAKES A COUNTRY GREAT

If the Chinese have lost the historically unique opportunity appeared in the beginning of this century, through which China would become a world power or would play an important role in international affairs as many Chinese dreamed and are dreaming, then it means that a country can seize an opportunity, which can be either an internal opportunity or an external opportunity, to stand out. Nevertheless, the opportunity for the Chinese at the beginning of this century is an external opportunity, because the Chinese have already successfully caught the internal opportunity and is becoming an economic power at world stage.

In such a context, I asked myself what makes a country great, although one might exemplify uncountable factors to make a country great, this would not be the way to establish a concept accessible and analytical.

2.1 THRESHOLD

For the appearance at world stage, it seems to be the common knowledge that the size of country and size of population are not significant contributors to the becoming of great country, as the US population is about 6% of world population, but she dominates the world affairs since the end of Word War II. By clear contrast, Chinese and Indians contribute a significant portion of world population, but play a rather small role at international stage.

However, the population size and country size do play a great role at world stage, at least we need to admit that there is a threshold for a country to be important at world stage.

I would suggest to set this threshold as the size of Cuba or Korea with population larger than 10 millions of people. In such a definition, Israel is not able to be a world power although she is a regional power and the Jewish people contribute significantly to the world civilization. With this size of country and population, a country can have a lasting image at world stage. For example, the Latin music and sportsmen from Cuba is labeled as coming from Cuba, but the culture from Jewish people is not labeled as coming from Israel. Still, the nuclear programs in North Korea and Libya would be considered somewhat similar, but the attention given to both countries is different although Libya has more resource than North Korea, because I would suggest that the population size of Libya is less than 10-million people threshold. Another example is Yugoslavia, which passed the 10-million people threshold and appeared at world stage, and current ex-Yugoslavia countries, each has the population less than 10 millions, and could not appear at world stage. Still Hungary and Portugal are two countries with their population size larger than 10 millions, and had appeared at the world stage. I would suggest that Georgia as an independent country is far below this threshold, which means that it is hard for Georgia to debut at world stage. In fact, if a country is too small, her history and culture is difficult to spread out to the world although this history might be very rich.

Likely, this threshold is the way to keep the nation identity from a national identity. Another threshold, which I would suggest, would be the population size about 50 millions of people, which are the size of European powers with reference to history and the size of current G 8 countries except for Canada, and this threshold would be the threshold for a country to maintain her long-term stay at world stage.

I would suggest that Ukraine is just below this threshold although Ukraine people once dreamed to be the second France with somewhat similar population size and country size, when she declared her independence as I was studying in Moscow, Russia. I would also suggest that the population size of Taiwan is far below this threshold, which implies that Taiwan cannot stay at world stage for a long period as we had seen her departure from the UN in 1971. Still, I would suggest that a united Korea would pass this threshold easily. This is to say that a united Korea could stay at world stage in long-term trend if she has such a will. This might also suggest why the major world powers would like to see a separate Korea, because a united Korea equipped with nuclear weapons would endanger the world.

Certainly, now the size of population and size of country would play a far more important role for a country to appear at world stage because the successful development of capitalism, which gives everyone a more or less view from stock market. That is to say that an investor should look at the potential of stock, similarly, more and more people look at a country from the investor's viewpoint, namely, the larger is the population size, the larger is the country size, the larger is the potential to make more money. Therefore the size of population and size of country is no longer unimportant as many people previously thought.

2.2 Life in Great Country and Small Kingdom

As China easily passes these two thresholds defined in the above section, so China would have a good potential to stay long at world stage, which could be considered a marker as a great country if we would like to think so. Actually many countries pass the two thresholds defined above, these countries like China are still far away from a world power. For this phenomenon, I would suggest that the people, who live in these potential-world-power countries, conduct a life, which belongs to a small kingdom.

Until May 1, 2008, the UN has 192 members [7], while only 51 nations attended the first meetings of the General Assembly of UN in 40s in 20th century [8]. Although the historians and politicians would say that this is the evidence that more and more countries want to be independent, I would suggest that this is the evidence that more and more people prefer the life in a small kingdom or people spontaneously hope to live in a small kingdom, whose borders and sovereignty are guaranteed by international laws or treaty and world powers.

A question raised here is why people like the life in a small kingdom although everyone hopes her/his country to be a world power? The simplest answer is that the life in a small kingdom is very much comfortable.

In physics, more concrete, in thermodynamics, there is a term, entropy, saying that spontaneous changes in isolated system occur with an increase in entropy, and spontaneous changes tend to smooth out differences in temperature, pressure, density and chemical potential that exist in a system [9]. If we use a Chinese proverb, that is, the water always moves to a lower place.

Similarly, we, humans, would spontaneously go back to our original desires when we live in a place, which is isolated from outside world, see, how many couples dream to live in a small island without any other human being. Perhaps, our original desires would be what we dream as indicated by Sigmund Freud's psychoanalysis [10]. In other words, the entropy of our original desires would increase when we live in an isolate place.

Now let us throw away these abstract concepts of entropy and psychoanalysis, but look at the real life in great country and small kingdom.

The simplest way to determine if the life is comfortable is to count how many holidays in the country of interest. China had the following holidays in 2008:

[1] New Year holiday: one day was designed as an official holiday, after adjusted with other days, and the actually holidays were 3 days.
[2] Chinese New Year (Spring Festival): three days were designed as official holidays, after adjusted with other days, and the actual holidays were 7 days.
[3] Tomb-sweeping Day: one day was designed as an official holiday after adjusted with other days, and the actual holidays were 3 days.
[4] May Day: one day was designed as an official holiday after adjusted with other days, and the actual holidays were 3 days.
[5] Dragon boat festival: one day was designed as an official holiday after adjusted with other days, and the actual holidays were 3 days.
[6] Mid-autumn festival: one day was designed as an official holiday after adjusted with other days, the actual holidays were 3 days.
[7] National Day: three days were designed as an official holiday after adjusted with other days, and the actual holidays were 7 days.

Actually the Chinese also have a number of rather small or local holidays, which need celebration and rest in reference to the Chinese calendar, such as festival of lanterns, international women's day, children's day, Chinese valentine's day, evil's day, double ninth (September 9 in Chinese calendar), etc.

Besides, the Chinese currently mark almost all famous holidays used in western world and the US, for example, carnival, valentine's day, April day, Easter, mother's day, father's day, Halloween, thanksgiving day, Christmas, etc. The Chinese people enjoy the life during these holidays, although no official holidays are assigned. In fact, the Christmas is a big sale event in China, though most of Chinese are not followers of this religion, each place is decorated with Christmas tree and Santa Claus.

By the measure of holidays, I would say that the Chinese have more holidays in their peaceful, stable and development periods, when they really have few things to worry.

Traditionally China does not have many restrictions and limits besides several particular historical periods, and the following is the observation made by non-Chinese one hundred years ago [3]:

"Every one who has lived in China, and has kept his eyes open, must have noticed what a large measure of personal freedom is enjoyed by even the meanest subject of the Son of Heaven. Any Chinaman may travel all over China without asking any one's leave to start, and without having to report himself, or be reported by his innkeeper, at any place at which he may choose to stop. He requires no passport. He may set up any legitimate business at any place. He is not even obliged to be educated, or to follow any particular calling. He is not obliged to serve as a soldier or sailor. There are no sumptuary laws, nor even any municipal laws. . . So long as a man keeps clear of secret societies and remains a decent and respectable member of his family and of his clan, he has very little to fear from the officials."

Thus, the current data and historical narrative strongly suggest that the life in China is quite comfortable, even more comfortable than the people in other countries.

When looking at the Chinese history again, the most interesting and fascinating period would be the dynasty Zhou, 1122 BC - 256 BC, including Spring and Autumn period and Warring States period. The historical fiction [11] does suggest that the people lived in a small kingdom have a better life than the people live in a big kingdom, simply because neither king nor ordinary people care anything occurred outside their small kingdom, either they have no ability to deal with the affairs occurred outside their small kingdom or they have no interest in the affairs occurred outside their small kingdom. Thus the life in these small kingdoms is just relaxing, playing, loving, eating, sexing, until these small kingdoms were conquered by another bigger kingdom.

In the sense of entropy, I would suggest that the comfortable life is more or less related to an isolated place, or a country isolated from outside world. This is very the case for most periods of Chinese history, and China is arguably a small kingdom in this sense.

One might argue that the example above in Chinese history is more related to the small-size kingdoms, in fact, a big-size kingdom can well behave as a small-size kingdom does, whose final fate is very simple, conquered by another big-size kingdom. In Chinese history, kingdom Qi was destroyed in such a way. Then there are two equal big-size kingdoms, Qin and Qi, and four other small-size kingdoms. Kingdom Qin wanted to conquer these five kingdoms and unite China, however her military power is far smaller than the sum of these five kingdoms together, especially kingdom Qi plays a balancing role. With the conspiracy suggested by various staffs, kingdom Qin successfully made kingdom Qi enjoy the leisure life and not care what happened outside her big-size kingdom, and finally all these five kingdoms were conquered by kingdom Qin with a united China [11].

In the ancient time, the small kingdom sooner or later would belong to other big kingdoms, why did people in small kingdom not enjoy their life for a moment? This is the underlined philosophy.

Hong Kong and South Korea have tremendous influence on the Chinese daily life since the beginning of reform in China. They are the examples for many Chinese to follow in some sense.

Although I have suggested that a united Korea would stay at world stage for a long period, the history shows that Korea is not the case. Actually the Korea's situation is somewhat similar to Poland, which is located between two powerful countries, Russia and Germany. Therefore the biggest ambition for a country in such a terribly geological location is to be independent. Indeed, Korea was far better than Poland because the Chinese are not as aggressive as Russians and Germans in history, but Korean first dream is still independent of China and Japan, the second dream would be to enjoy life before slaved in ancient time, colonized for the last two centuries and lost of national identity in modern history. The ambition of Hong Kong is far smaller than Korea, if not zero, because Hong Kong has no identity, besides enjoyment. The life in Hong Kong is purely the life in small kingdom. Thus the influence from Hong Kong and South Korea could prevent Chinese from having a great ambition of becoming of a world power.

On the other hand, the history shows that the kings lived in a big kingdom are always worrying and thinking how to conquer small kingdoms. This thought requires either the people in a big kingdom to think as same as their kings or the people to live in less comfortable way in order to prepare a war or work hard to make more money available for a war.

In Chinese history, two famous prime ministers, Guan Zhong (725 BC – 645 BC) and Shang Yang (died 338 BC), had separately told Duke Huan of Qi (died 643 BC) and Duke Xiao of Qin (381 BC – 338 BC) that the ordinary people are satisfied with current situation, and do not want any changes, etc [11]. These mean that the ordinary people have trend to conduct the life in small kingdom.

The modern history shows that the life in great country seems not to be so comfortable, because the great country has so many world or regional entitlements that her people have to contribute to these entitlements, although the citizens from a great country could be very proud when they travel in small kingdoms.

When I arrived at USSR in the end of 80s of last century, people frequently and generally considered that the hardship in ordinary people's daily life was due to the entitlement of Soviet Union, because her money spent on supporting world revolutions.

The source, which I forgot, says that Mao Zedong once asked the cost of development of nuclear weapon, and someone answered that it would cost the money for a war. Accordingly I would suggest that the poorly economic condition in North Korea, which is laughed by many Chinese, is mainly due to the development of her nuclear program as North Korea was once richer than South Korea [12]. The latter does not need to spend so much money on her defense because the treaty with the US guarantees her sovereignty.

Therefore, without world entitlement and national ambition, the life in small kingdom would be far more comfortable than the life in great country, whose money spends on military establishment, defense of small kingdom, various treaties, etc.

Historically, China is quite isolated, not only because her language is too difficult to communicate with other cultures, but also because of the geographical location of China as the Himalayas blocks communication between China and India, the Gobi desert blocks China and Central Asia, and the Siberia blocks China and Europe. Thus, China is quite isolated in her history, and would spontaneously and automatically go to the life in a small kingdom, which does not care anything outside her border, even does not know what happens outside her border. In fact it was impossible to know the outside world if we consider the technology at that time, so China traditionally behaves as a small kingdom.

In this view, the name of China is also very suggestive: China sometimes is named as Middle Kingdom, which could be explained as that behavior of Chinese is between a great country and a small kingdom, some Chinese hope China to be a great country, some Chinese hope to conduct a life in small kingdom. The mixture is the Middle Kingdom.

Finally, I would suggest that the American people conducted the life in small kingdom before World War II, as we read that McGeorge Bundy refused to answer the essay questions on summer vacations or favorite pets, instead writing on how inane the topics were, on his college-board exam [13, 14]. Clearly, the essay presents the mainstream of American society at that time, enjoying of summer vacation and pets.

2.3 What Makes a Country Great

If a country, after passing two defined thresholds, does not conduct a small-kingdom life, then what she needs to do to become a world power?

At this stage, I would argue that generally there are at least three ways to make a country great, (i) application of a great systematical thought, (ii) entitlement, and (iii) opportunity.

Of course, it would be extremely lucky for a country if she has these three ways together and simultaneously. However, the modern history does show such a case, for example, the US had simultaneously such three ways together after World War II, (i) the US democracy and freedom, (ii) her economic and military power, and (iii) the vacuum left after World War II. At the same period, the Soviet Union did simultaneously have such three ways together after World War II, (i) the Marxism-Leninism and communism, (ii) her military power, and economic power at 70s of last century, and (iii) the vacuum left after World War II.

Taking a step back, I would suggest that the combination of any two ways would be also very lucky for a country. I might suggest that Cuba is such an example, she has the legendary Che Guevara as a model of thought, and her world communism entitlement as shown her military missions in Afraica during 60s-70s of last century.

2.3.1 Application of a Great Systematical Thought

Here, the systematical thought must be the thought directly related to all mankind in this planet. This thought can be either a pure dream, for example, Utopia [15], or a nightmare, for example, nuclear war, star war [16], but it must be oriented to all humans, especially it must deal with the distribution of social wealth and the exercise of social justice. The key point is to attract world for a very long period.

In general, the origination of systematical thoughts is more likely to belong to an individual activity without a large-scale social effort, or without the commission of government. Actually the application of a great thought is more easily to make a country great than the production of a great systematical thought by an individual. For example, the BBC poll indicates that Karl Marx is the greatest thinker for the last millennium [17], which only makes Karl Marx himself great, but the application of Marxism made the USSR great. Thus, it is likely that the modern history is the history that a country can outstand with a new idea or an ideological concept.

The reason for the Soviet Union to become a superpower is the Leninism, which, based on Marxism, calling for building a new social system. Actually, the Soviet Union was the model for all the socialist countries. During 50s of 20th century the slogan in China was that today's Soviet Union would be tomorrow's China, and everyone called Soviet Union as a big brother.

The reason for the UK to become a great country is her colonialism with her superior in sciences, technology and her leading role in industrial revolution. In fact, the UK had a wide spectrum of thoughts from science to literature, which laid the advanced positions at that time.

The reason for modern France to become a great country is her Liberté, Égalité and Fraternité, and her independent thoughts during the time of Charles de Gaulle. For example, he withdrew France from the NATO military command, he objected to Britain's entry into the European Community, he recognized the People's Republic of China [18] and and he acted independently in international affairs.

The reason for morden US to become the model to follow and the dreamland for most people is her demoncracy, freedom, oppotunity provided to each person.

Likely, the Nazi grows up based on the unhappiness for the results of World War I and National Socialism, nationalism, etc.

. . .

Hence, to be a great country, it must have something extremely attracting outside world. Although there are many issues, which can attract outside world, such as economy, living standard, investment opportunity, culture, etc., the most important is if there is a thinking leader, who creates a new system of thinking for that era and future for the mankind.

I would argue the main cause, which leads a country to become a powerful country, even a superpower country, is the new idea, a systematical thought. This is especially true over last three hundred years, because there are constantly new means to distribute the new ideas or new system of thoughts.

The historical trend suggests that China has little chance to produce such a thought although the Chinese current model in economic development could be attractive.

In Chinese history, China exported extremely few thoughts related to the distribution of social wealth and the exercise of social justice, if not none. Once the Maoism has prevailed in the third world, but the Maoism has been related to the later life of Mao Zedong, leading the reduction of popularity of Maoism. From this viewpoint, I would suggest that the Chinese would have an extremely great difficulty in producing a systematical thought related to all mankind. Perhaps, this is one reason why the Chinese language is not attractive, because it does not carry any great thoughts related to all mankind.

2.3.2 Regional and World Entitlement

In some sense, the entitlement requires a country to have a suitably economic and military power, which cannot be achieved within days, weeks, months, years, even decades.

Doubtless, the US has such a world entitlement, because the US economy currently is about 23% world economy [19]. The analysis according to the Lanchester's equation on market share defines that if each player shares less than 7% in a market, then there is no trend in this market. A market player can lead, dominate and control a market if it has about 26.1%, 41.7% and 73.9% shares [20]. Of course, these figures should not be treated as an exact law, but 25%, 50% and 75% would be reasonable figures to account for the role in world economy, that is, the US still leads the trend of world economy. With such a leading role in world economy, the US has a strong world entitlement.

With her economic and military power, Israel has a strong entitlement in Middle East, which is a regional entitlement.

When looking around other world powers, I would suggest that Japan would play some role in world entitlement, not only because her economy is still relatively large, but also Japan has a strong military history among all Asian countries. Perhaps, Japan is the only country in Asia, which has not been colonized during Asian history, while this fact is very different from other Asian countries, which were colonized in 19th and 20th centuries. Historically, European countries have more world entitlements than the countries in Asia and Africa.

Perhaps with the increase in economic might, the countries from Asia, Africa and Latin America would have more world entitlements, however this hypothesis should be put with a question mark, because these countries are still not used to consider the world affair independently.

In this context, China is difficult to have a great world entitlement, not only because Chinese economy is relatively small, which is still far less than the dominated ratio defined by Lanchster's equation [20], but also the Chinese army never really goes far beyond Chinese border. In Chinese history, the Chinese army had few successes to completely defeat the invaders.

In this sense, the issue of whether a country is great or not is directly related to her entitlement in the world rather than the population size, territory size, civilization, etc.

Based on the above arguments, I would suggest that a country would be great if she assumes her world entitlement, or her mission is oriented to the outside world, although these world entitlements might suggest the preemptive doctrine.

2.3.3 Opportunity

An old Chinese proverb says: "tian shi, di li, ren he". This proverb can be understood and translated as follows: the opportunity provided by god or the timing of opportunity, the geographic advantage, and the peace between people.

In some sense, this Chinese proverb is equivalent to the common saying that to do right thing at right time in right place, however the difference between Chinese and non-Chinese in these two sayings is that the Chinese consider the human factor.

All these two sayings suggest the importance of opportunity, so a country can relatively easily use an opportunity to change her image. At international stage, the country's image is mainly related to political and economic images. The economic image generally needs years to change, but the political image can be changed overnight.

Although I would suggest that the easiest way for a country to debut is to go through a political way with the internal focus on an issue related to this debut, it requires the country prepared. Perhaps, the most difficult point is how we can define an opportunity, because no country can catch an opportunity without clear definition of what an opportunity is. More scientifically I would suggest how to measure an opportunity, then we would have the possibility of taking the advantage from the opportunity. Actually no one has defined the first several years in 21st century as a historically unique opportunity for China.

However, the biggest difficulty related to opportunity is that it is almost unpredictable, especially the opportunity with high impact, otherwise it would not be called as opportunity, but commonplace.

At internationally political stage, the opportunity is generally related to the change of regimes, or change of leaders or deaths of leaders, which are somewhat predictable, because there would always be signs on these events. Besides, the opportunity at international level is generally not an overnight opportunity, which is usable for a period of time.

Another equally important issue is if the country has sufficient means to take the advantage from the defined opportunity In this capitalized world, the money is the means to some extent to take the advantage from an opportunity, thus I would suggest that Asian countries would have such a ability to debut at world stage, because these countries have too much money to know how to spend efficiently.

Theoretically, the opportunity would be an easy way for China to become a world power, if she is prepared. The problem for China is that the Chinese people are generally not sensitive to and slowly react to the events occurred outside

China, that is, the Chinese are internal-oriented while European and Americans are more external-oriented.

Chapter 3

CHINESE WAY OF THINKING

If the Chinese cannot produce any systematical theories related to all mankind on distribution of social wealth and exercise of social justice, do not have the inherited concept on regional and world entitlements, cannot see the opportunity at world stage, but prefer to conduct the life in small kingdom, then it is absolutely clear that the Chinese have their own way of thinking, which is disassociated from the requests to become a world power.

For this view, we need to examine what seems to be different in Chinese, their ways of thinking and living.

3.1 CHINESE PEOPLE

After studying and working in six different countries, Ukraine, Russia, Japan, Italy, France and Switzerland, for 14 years, I do not particularly feel how the Chinese are much uglier than other nationals, although the Chinese indeed have various weakness indicated by Bo Yang in his book "The Ugly Chinaman" [1].

In historical fiction [11], Duke Huan of Qi (died 643 BC) asked his prime minister Guan Zhong (725 BC – 645 BC): "I have two weaknesses, lechery and hunting for pleasure, I wonder if these two weaknesses prevent kingdom Qi from becoming a great state?" Guan Zhong answered: "No!, . . .". Similarly, the weaknesses indicated by Bo Yang do not prevent China from becoming a great country.

When working in Japan, a Chinese told me that she/he feels that the characteristics of Chinese are similar to that of Americans, and then she/he raised several simple examples to prove her/his points. Still a Russian colleague once told me people are the same in Moscow.

No matter whether their views are limited or biased. These views suggested that the difference between Chinese and non-Chinese could be as small as saying to be similar, or could be as big as indicated by Bo Yang in his book [1]. Clearly, this is a very personal view dependent on from where to look at the facts, although each national must have her identity associated with her natural surroundings. I believe that at personal level, people should be same or similar.

Clearly, there are many ways to estimate a national, for example, we can analyze if a national has any important contribution to human civilization, if a national has left a rich and great culture and tradition, if a national has significantly advanced human science and technology, etc.

However these measures are still more or less related to the personal contributions rather than the measures at national level, because I would argue that the above estimations are generally related to what a national does spontaneously during her history. In that case, the main contributions to human civilization are more or less attributed to the random contributions from individuals.

However, the humans have already advanced to such a stage that the role of random contributions from individuals becomes more and more difficult, because the government, big cooperation, and various organizations changed the random behavior of humans to a collective or cooperated effort on particular tasks.

Perhaps, the more scientific estimate on a national would evaluate if a national can do her best to reach the goal, which can be defined by the given country or is imposed by external forces: if a national has the ability to accomplish a task, which cannot be accomplished in any normal sense. If a national can sacrifice everything for her goal, then this national should get a higher score than other nationals in this aspect. My argument is that a national would like to suffer heavily, do everything and sacrifice everything to reach her goals.

The Chinese history suggests that the Chinese have such a great sacrificing spirit for the building of Great Wall, for the overthrowing of old dynasty, for example. However I have to admit that the Chinese had less sacrificing spirit during the war against foreign invaders besides the short periods in 20th century, because there are several quite long episodes in Chinese history that China is governed by non-Chinese, for example, the last dynasty Qing.

By clear contrast, I would suggest that many other nationals demonstrate a great sacrificing spirit in their history to defend their countries against foreign invaders, for example, Winston Churchill says [21]: "We shall fight in France, we shall fight on the seas and oceans, we shall fight with growing confidence and growing strength in the air, we shall defend our island, whatever the cost may be, we shall fight on the beaches, we shall fight on the landing grounds, we shall fight in the fields and in the streets, we shall fight in the hills; we shall never surrender." Similarly, Russians also demonstrated a great sacrificing spirit during her defense against Napoleon's invasion and Nazi's invasion.

"Whatever the cost may be" is generally different from traditionally Chinese view. This difference could be due to the Chinese philosophy, which does not care anything as Confucius said [22]: "If I do not drink I become a Buddha. If I drink I become an Immortal. Well, if there is wine, I shall drink; if there is none, I shall abstain." For this reasoning, I would suggest that the Chinese people perhaps very well evolved, that is, they can suit to any favorable and unfavorable situation no matter if China is governed by Chinese or non-Chinese. Or I would suggest that the Chinese people are too reasonable, as said by George Bernard Shaw [23]: "The reasonable man adapts himself to the world; the unreasonable one persists in trying to adapt the world to himself. Therefore, all progress depends on the unreasonable man." This could also provide the argument that the Chinese cannot make too much progress at world stage because they are too reasonable.

On the other hand, the Chinese have a great spirit of burdening the great suffer as documented by western churchman [24]. In fact, through Chinese history, we can find that many, even too many Chinese sacrificed for a great goal although the Chinese are less resistant to foreign invaders.

With this measure, that is, a national can sacrifice everything to reach her goal, I would suggest that the Chinese are not as ugly as Bo Yang defined although I do admit the weakness indicated by Bo Yang [1].

3.2 Thinking Pattern of Chinese

If the Chinese as a national do have the sprit of sacrificing everything to reach a defined goal, then it would be a dilemma of why the Chinese with such dear characteristics cannot use the opportunities appeared in front throughout history.

This again may be related to the valuation system of each national, however the valuation system is the result from thinking, there must be different ways of thinking to result in different valuation systems.

The thinking pattern can be found through one's behavior, thus we can observe the behavior of Chinese to get their thinking pattern. In Giles' lecture [3], he describes what the westerners saw the Chinese when they arrived at China in 19th century: "There was a time when China was regarded as a Land of Opposites, i.e. diametrically opposed to us in every imaginable direction. For instance, in China the left hand is the place of honor; men keep their hats on in company; use fans; mount their horses on the off side; begin dinner with fruit and end it with soup; shake their own instead of their friends' hands when meeting; begin at what we call the wrong end of a book and read from right to left down vertical columns; wear white for mourning; have huge visiting-cards instead of small ones; prevent criminals from having their hair cut; regard the south as the standard point of compass; begin to build a house by putting on the roof first; . . ."

All these observations only indicate that the Chinese civilization developed completely independently of outside world. I got a similar feeling when I first arrived in Japan and the UK, where I feel the different atmosphere from Asian and European continents. This only means that the civilization in Japan and the UK developed relatively independently, because then there were no efficient means to communicate between Asian continent and Japan, and between European continent and the UK. Therefore, the people living in Asian and European continents might have difficulty to understand the behavior as well as thoughts of people from Japan and the UK, and vice visa.

The different behaviors would suggest the different thinking patterns between Chinese and non-Chinese, the behavior of modern Chinese would be very different from the observation made in two hundred years ago or there is no big difference between Chinese and non-Chinese when using modern equipments, that is, the Chinese cannot put the roof first for any modern buildings in Shanghai and Beijing.

Likely the thinking pattern is not as important as we first glance at it, because the thinking pattern is only the pathway to reach a certain goal. However, the thinking pattern would be more associated with something occurred at genetic level, which could not be changed so easily.

Thus, I would suggest that the thinking pattern in Chinese is still opposite to non-Chinese, especially still is totally different from westerners in many ways. Now let us see some comparisons one by one at national level.

Western countries adopt the preemptive doctrine, while the Chinese adopt [25]: "I do not dare to be the host (to commence the war); I prefer to be the guest (to act on the defensive). I do not dare to advance an inch; I prefer to retire a foot".

A Chinese proverb says: "to have fewer disputes (things) is better than to have another more". Thus the Chinese generally are not interested in being involved in controversial issues as another Chinese proverb say: "to clean snow only in front of my door". By contrast, the westerners are more likely to raise the controversial issues, for example, the US Senate and Congress frequently discuss the issues occurred in other countries, while French passed the resolution on Armenian genocide.

If we compare the difference between Chinese and non-Chinese at personal level, we could see more differences, which might not be worthy listing one by one. However, the thinking pattern is in fact a spontaneous process without interference.

3.3 WHAT CHINESE THINK

If the pathway of thinking is the way to reach the goal, then we must see what is the final goal of Chinese thinking for most Chinese. In general, the Chinese do not like to think something very abstractive, but like to think something very much practical, very much related to personal life.

The following is mentioned in Hong Kong radio, a presenter on music program went to work by bus. In bus he heard the conversation of an old couple on the US election in 2008: this couple at first asked each other how much Obama would earn as a US president, then they agreed that Obama would not worry his retired life after his presidency because he would have a big pension, finally they discussed what pet Obama family would bring into the White House [26].

This perhaps could be the best sample of what the Chinese think during their daily life. In fact, the final goal of Chinese thinking generally reaches to the time of retirement, which means that the Chinese are not shortsighted but great far-sighted. For my personal experience, I got a lot of advices when I finished my middle school. Almost all the advice went on in such a way: I should do my best to be assigned to work in a state-owned factory rather than in a collective factory because the job was assigned at that time. The reason is very practical and simple: the pension would be equal to my salary when I would be retired from a state-owned factory but the pension would be a portion of my salary when I would be retired from a collective factory. In fact, I had no way to determine where I could go to work because we were assigned jobs in 70s of last century, more interestingly then I was less than 18-year old, but people already planed my retirement. Ironically, when I met my classmates in state-owned factory in 90s of last century, these classmates complained me how the life was difficult in state-owned factory because the reform in China changed the planned economy to market economy, and how lucky they would be if they would have been assigned in a collective factory in 70s of last century, because many private factories worked well in 90s.

So we cannot say that the Chinese are shortsighted people because they design their life from childhood. Their hope in fact is very simple, to work and to have money when they are old. During the revolutionary years, there is such a proverb mentioning the goal of Chinese people: to have a 2-hectare land, a cow, a wife, children and warm kang (bed) at home. Of course, this proverb satirized this type of thought belonging to peasants during the revolutionary years.

In a Chinese classical novel, whose name I cannot remember by now, it says that an intellectual has three goals in his life, (i) a good living room, (ii) a good bed, and (iii) a good coffin. There is another Chinese proverb saying the four issues in human life: (i) birth, (ii) old, (iii) disease and (iv) death. These could be the endpoint for most Chinese meditation.

For another example, which was positively praised by a presenter in Hong Kong radio several years ago, the presenter told us how to choose a son-in-law, the method actually is simple, even very trivial, to see if a son-in-law candidate is capable of frying a fish correctly, because the technique of frying of fish is very delicate and this son-in-law candidate should have a great patience to do it well.

Interestingly, one of great Chinese sage, Lao Tzu (Tsu), says it with different implication: "Governing a great state is like cooking a small fish." [25].

Clearly, the focus of Chinese thought is much very concentrated to themselves without any concerns on outside world. This type of thoughts are very common in European fables and tales, where a girl meets a prince, then they get married, have a lot of children and live happily until the end of their life. In such a comparison, I would suggest that the goal of thinking in most Chinese is still equal to the level of early stage of development of mankind.

Actually, when we look back to human history, we can find that the promises in each revolution or social changes are quite similar, that is, the politicians offer (i) jobs, (ii) free education, (iii) free medical care, and (iv) reassuring retirement. However, these aims are still not met in any social structure.

Of course, I would suggest that these goals are the goals in long-term trend in Chinese history, most likely to occur during the peaceful time in Chinese history. However, the goal in short-term trend can be very different from the goal in long-term trend if the life in short-term become unbearable. However, the goal in short-term trend is unlikely to continue more than two or three generations to give up to the goal in long-term trend, that is very simple, to have more funs during lifetime, money, love, face value, etc. The country is generally feminized, as demonstrated in literature and Chinese society.

3.4 WHAT IS CHINESE SPIRIT

At this moment one might ask what is a national spirit, and what is the Chinese spirit. I would suggest that the goal and thinking pattern in long-term trend would be the national spirit.

For Japanese, everyone would say hagakure, which is indeed the long-term trend although becomes less intensive recently than before. Broadly speaking, I would suggest that the national spirit is more related to the national pride. For Japanese example again, it is well known that there are various writings, generally dirty words, on walls in almost all the public toilets. In 1993, in Kumamoto, Japan, I saw such a sentence on the wall in a public toilet, say, "Please do not write any thing on the wall, it is a shame of Japanese!" Perhaps this is a sample of the Japanese spirit, their national pride. Another my personal experience on Japanese national pride is when I first arrived at Narita international airport in 1993, I asked a porter where is Tokyo, he very proudly pointed to a direction just beyond horizon saying: "There, the number one in the world!".

Perhaps, this spirit made Japan is perhaps the only country in Asia without colonized land, while non-Asians generally colonized other countries in Asia although China was partly colonized in 19th century. Perhaps, the generally weak history in Asia could be partly attributed to the popularity of Buddhism in Asia, which compromises and adopts a passive attitude to resist to new ideas. Although Japanese follow Buddhism, their particular thought makes the Buddhism less important than the existence of national.

Once a British asked me that she/he felt it strange because the Chinese have no intention against non-Chinese who work in China, and the Chinese never consider that these non-Chinese affect their job opportunities, however, this would be a severe problem of economic immigration in any European countries.

In this context, it is likely that the Chinese spirit has little nationalism and national pride because Chinese history shows far less intensive and active military war against non-Chinese invaders or passive resistance against non-Chinese governors. Perhaps, the Chinese follow the ancient Chinese sage too closely, who says [25]: "There is no guilt greater than to sanction ambition".

However, I would suggest that the trend of national pride is becoming less clear because the new world powers brought in the new ideas, new technology, and new life style, which the Chinese accept without hesitation, even all the Asian countries, which are contrast to the strong resistance found in Islam world.

Once, one of my relatives told me that a man should give up his duty and ambition to please the woman he loves. This made me recall the poem, which was once popular in China and suggested written by Hungarian poet Petofi Sandor, although I could not find the English version, I could translate this poem as follows: "Life is valuable / Love is more valuable / However I can give them up for freedom." The time this poem was popular is the time of Chinese revolution, while now we can read such analysis on this poem, that is, what is the meaning of freedom if one loses his life [27].

Hence, it is highly likely that the Chinese spirit in a long-term trend is the traditional four Chinese words, eating, drinking, playing and enjoying pleasure.

Chapter 4

WHAT CHINESE LACK

If the Chinese spirit in a long-term trend is just eating, drinking, playing and enjoying pleasure, which are in fact the basic needs at the lowest level of humans, then the Chinese people would lack something at high level, which could make them become an influential and great country.

Among three factors defined in previous chapters, systematical theory, entitlement and opportunity, the opportunity would occur outside of China, the entitlement would also occur outside of China, but only the systematical theory would come inside China.

In this context, I would suggest that the Chinese lack great thinkers, who can formulate a systematical theory, which would bring the breakthrough in distribution of social wealth and exercise of social justice, would attract millions of people to follow around the world.

Actually there are many, many very talent, even extremely very talent people in Chinese history, whose ideas were extremely smart, however, these smart ideas did not spread widely, because these ideas were unfortunately not systematically formulated. As people often say that good ideas are everywhere, but worthless.

Perhaps, it is only the systematically formulated theory that has the power to spread widely and has the influence on millions of people around the world, while a single piece of smart idea cannot distribute far before buried by huge amount of information. It is only a systematical theory, which can raise a series of reasoning and stand up with time.

In fact, the Chinese language cannot spread around world, not only because it is hard to learn, but also the most important is that the Chinese language does not carry great thoughts and systematical theories. I do not consider it more difficult to learn the Chinese language than to learn Greek and Latin in ancient time, when there were no dictionaries, no sound records, almost nothings. Thus China basically does not export thoughts, which are proportional to her population size and territorial size.

Too many examples show that the Chinese people could be good at tricks and tip, but not good at systematical thoughts. There is a famous Chinese proverb, even perhaps world proverb, to live until very old, to study until very old, or never too old to study. This suggests that people are more interested in the absorption of knowledge, but not creation of idea, which perhaps is one of most traditional Chinese thoughts.

I would suggest that the reason why Europe has been the center of the world for so long time is that Europeans produce so many thoughts and theories, which help humans to explore the universe and themselves.

4.1 Systematical Theory

Great thinkers would produce systematical theories on various topics. The simplest measure is to see how many –isms produced by Chinese. When looking around, we could find few –ism originated from China.

For example, there were more than 870 items of –isms under the entry of List of belief systems in Current version of Wikipedia (updated to the end of November of 2008), and about 210 items of –isms on The Ism Book [28], however only few came from China.

Meanwhile, the definition of –ism in Wikipedia is as follows: the suffix -ism denotes a distinctive system of beliefs, myth, doctrine or theory that guides a social movement, institution, class or group. Therefore the fact is that the Chinese produce far less widely recognized –isms than other nationals or the ratio of production of –ism is not proportional to the size of Chinese population.

In fact, the Chinese people are very weak in making a new theory although they have many brilliant ideas, and most Chinese theories do not come from analysis but from dream or meditations or imaginations. Sometimes my experience as a reviewer suggests that the Chinese could not distinguish a small modification of current theory from the creation of new theory, i.e. the authors in their manuscripts always claim that they developed a new approach, but the reality is that they just modify a little in the current approach.

4.1.1 Religion

In ancient time, perhaps the most systematical theory would be religion. If we look at the most popular religions in the world, three profound religions are Christianity, Buddhism and Islam, I would suggest that the Chinese did not contribute anything significant to these three religions although Buddhism was very popular in China for a considerable time. These three religions are really systematical theories.

In Chinese history, the Taoism is generally viewed as a religion, which, although praised by Chinese for thousands of yours, is not a systematical theory I would argue. This is so because it does not include (i) a religious figure, whose personality is fascinating, (ii) a religious goal, i.e. paradise or hell, (iii) a religious worship, etc. Of course, it could not exclude the possibility that the Taoism appeared too earlier that humans might not have ability to make it a systematical theory. However, the history indicates that this type of religion cannot spread out around the world as a major religion.

Also, it could not exclude the possibility of minor religions developed in Chinese history, however, they had no ability to spread widely.

I have visited several Taoism temples in China, where a visitor can get a free booklet on Taoism sometimes, however this booklet contains only few pages of size A6 paper (4.1 × 5.8 inch, 105 × 148 mm), and each page contains few sentences. This is not a systematical religion, but slogans.

I would therefore suggest that the religion in China is a luxurious business rather than a serious belief. This is so because the religion becomes popular when China experiences a considerable time of development. For example, the famous Chinese classical novel, Journey to the West [29], describes the pursuit of Buddhism commissioned by the emperor Li Shiming, which is one of peaceful and best periods in Chinese history that I defined as the second opportunity in Chinese history to become a regional power.

Thus, the rise of religion in China is simply a show. This is to say that any religious ceremony has a single purpose to demonstrate that we are rich and can spend money for any purpose. Almost all the great temples were built for such a show, because we hardly see that any philanthropy in Chinese history was done related to the religion as Mother Teresa did. For example, there is no hospital run by any religious groups in China.

On the other hand, the religion in China is far more related to the various very practical aims in ordinary Chinese: how to find the secret to live longer, pray to have a boy to prolong a family line, pray the baby not to cry during the night, pray to make money in stock market, pray to win a lottery, etc. Actually I never see that anyone prays to save her/his soul, which deems to be the goal in other religions. In many Chinese temples, one can see such a sentence, "If you pray, you will get what you pray". However, the prayer only burns several joss sticks for the return of extremely hugely good luck or fortune, which is certainly impossible, if we consider the Newton's law "To every action there is an equal and opposite reaction." [30], in other words the leverage of a simple prayer would be too large to be true.

In chapter 34 of Chinese classical novel, Water Margin or Outlaws of the Marsh [31], we can read such an episode: "With 150 men, Huang Xin takes Song Jiang and Hua Rong to the prefect as prisoners. Along the way, they are stopped by the Clear Wind Mountain bandits numbering 500, who demand a toll [32]. Liu Gao prayed the god to save his life and his suffer, and he would read 100 000 volumes of scripture and build 300 temples if he would be saved. But finally Hua Rong kills Liu Gao."

In these cases, the religion in China is sometimes similar to magic, that is, when a person is in danger or in trouble or in need of something, he/she prays.

Still, we would hardly find any Chinese temple, where people conduct serious systematically scientific research and systematical meditation on any serious subjects. This only once again demonstrates that the religion in China is only a luxurious show.

Any luxurious business cannot construct any serious religion although there are sometimes many followers in a suddenly popular so-called religion in China. Perhaps, due to the fact that the Chinese are not used to systematical thoughts, thus a small idea can be labeled as a new religion with many followers. If we look around the world, we can find that there is no creation of major religions for a quite long time. This means that the human evolution makes the birth or creation of new religion become more difficult either because of the advance of science and technology or because of lack of great interests in creating a systematical religion.

In such a case, the birth of new religions in China is a practical joke, which goes against the long-term trend in the world. This is to say that it is almost impossible for a single person to create a new systematical religion at current stage of human knowledge. This is an underdevelopment sign of Chinese in analysis. Nevertheless, any religions created in China cannot spread widely.

4.1.2 Three Systematical Theories

Likely, the Chinese have created three major systematical theories of thought in Chinese history, the first would be the Taoism with several other sages, the second would be I Ching or Book of Changes, and the third would be the traditional Chinese medicine. Of course, this is based on my limited knowledge on Chinese history.

Frankly speaking, these three systematical theories came out far before the beginning of modern sciences. Therefore it is really sad that we, Chinese, have not made any big progress in creation of new systematical theory of thought over the last a thousand years. This might be attributed to the underdevelopment of China over last a thousand years. In such a case, one naturally wonders why three systematical theories did not spread around the world.

If we look at the theories created by ancient Chinese sages in comparison with other theories, which are popular around the world, we would bitterly admit that the Chinese theories are neither qualitative nor quantitative, even they are so obscure that we can have many different explanations with so-called great insight. For example, "the sage manages affairs without doing anything, and conveys his instructions without the use of speech" [25]. What does this sentence adored by generations of Chinese say? The best explanation I can give is that then humans had no means to manage a state, because there were no laws, no regulations, no governments, no political parties, no efficient communications, even no civilizations, etc., the best way should be to do nothing or in fact do not know what to do.

Sometimes, we find no definite solution in Chinese theory created by sages because their sentences can be explained in very different ways. The application of this type of theory, such as Tao Teh Ching, is an art rather than a clear cut-off technology. Besides, although the ancient Chinese sages provide great insights into life, I would honestly say that some blogs written by current generation of unknown young women and men are as insightful as these sages with respect to their thinking and philosophical implications. This is possible because the human knowledge in ancient China is very limited, what found by Chinese sages at that time was extremely great, but it appears little use and confused as human knowledge has advanced so much over last two thousand years.

Another possibility for the difficulty in understanding of ancient Chinese theories could be that the Chinese language had yet to well develop at that time, thus these sages had a great difficulty in expressing their deep thoughts, which are unclear according to the Chinese language developed at different historical times thereafter, thus we have endless annotations from generation to generation.

Similar feeling can be seen in several Amazon readers' comments on classic novel Robinson Crusoe [33]. For example, in "important only for its place in history" it reads [34]: " . . . 'Robinson Crusoe' was one of the first, if not the first modern novel. . . It is hard for a book written in 1717 to translate all that well into the 21st Century." In "Not For the Modern Reader" it reads [35]: "There are many people who believe that, if something is a 'first' or 'innovative' or 'influential' then it is necessarily great. Robinson Crusoe was in many ways a first, innovative and influential – no one can ever take that away from this book. . . Maybe this was a great book for the people in the eighteenth century who had never had the opportunity to read better novels, but to the modern era it falls very flat on a number of levels".

Another problem related to Chinese theory is that the measures suggested by sages seem to work on an unlimited time scale, which is indeed very hard to be applied to the real-life practice. Perhaps this is another reason why the Chinese theories do not spread far enough, of course, though the humans then had little concept on the time.

A far more mysterious theory created by ancient Chinese sage is I Ching or Book of Changes, and the humans have already spent so much time and energy on the explanations and implications of this book, but the clear and universally-agreed answer is still not got. This might simply suggest that the explanation of I Ching is somewhat similar to the Euclid's fifth postulate, which cannot be solved in Euclidean space [36], or beyond the human limit. Interestingly, Giles told us [3]: "One erratic genius of the West has gone so far as to say that it is only a vocabulary of the language of some old Central Asian tribe."

Perhaps, the most successful theory created by Chinese should be the traditional Chinese medicine. As my background is related to the Western medical sciences, my view on the transitional Chinese medicine could be biased. However, let me restate what a Chinese medical doctor discussed with me on the traditional Chinese medicine when I was an MD student. This discussion was done in 1984, however it impressed me so much that I cannot forget the great insight I got from this discussion.

I asked: "In your view, which is better, the traditional Chinese medicine or the Western medicine?"

She/He answered: "Surely, the traditional Chinese medicine is better, even the best!"

"Why?"

"It is very simple, a medical doctor always needs to learn something new if she/he studies the Western medicine because there are always new developments, big new developments in Western medicine. For example, a medical doctor did not need to know the meaning of X-ray diagnosis in the past because there were few X-ray machines, but now a medical doctor needs to know the meanings of X-ray diagnosis, CT diagnosis, type-B ultrasonic diagnosis, etc. Thus a medical doctor in Western medicine always has to learn new technologies, new clinical tests, new drugs, etc. In short, she/he needs to learn everything new in Western medicine.

"Do you mean that a medical doctor in traditional Chinese medicine does not need to learn any new technology?"

"They need, of course. But the difference is if a medical doctor in traditional Chinese medicine can understand 10% of what written a thousand years ago in ancient Chinese medical books, she/he would be a great expert in traditional Chinese medicine. For a medical doctor in Western medicine, even she/he has learnt 90% of what written now, she/he is still not an expert!"

"Yes?!"

"Besides, a medical doctor in traditional Chinese medicine is an easy-life job, even a leisure job."

"Why?"

"Why? If a patient would be in a crucial condition, her/his family members would automatically send the patient to a hospital equipped with Western medicine, for example, if a person breaks her/his leg, she/he would go to where she/he can get a quick treatment. By clear contrast, the patients, who come to the hospitals equipped with traditional Chinese medicine, are generally not in crucial conditions, their diseases are never sufficiently severe. Actually their disease are more or less related to the aging, poor health, psychological problem, etc., but not related to a specific pathogen. Thus the job for a medical doctor in traditional Chinese medicine is never in great hurry."

"Are there other benefits for a medical doctor in traditional Chinese medicine?"

"A lot, a lot!! For example, the patients, who visit a medical doctor in traditional Chinese medicine, generally are the people with some power, because the poor people have no time to treat these luxurious diseases, therefore a medical doctor in traditional Chinese medicine would know more powerful people than a medical doctor in Western medicine does. This is the major benefit for a medical doctor in traditional Chinese medicine."

"Is there other shortness for a medical doctor in Western medicine?"

"Yes, a lot, besides what I had said. For example, a medical doctor in Western medicine would have a bad interpersonal relationship with her/his colleagues, for example."

"Why?"

"A medical doctor in Western medicine, for example, I am a surgeon myself, has to conduct the operations when they appear necessary no matter daytime or night. Thus I have great problems with nurses as well as technicians, who do not like the ideas to conduct the operations at night or lunch or dinner time. I also have problems with cooks, because I frequently have to go to eat not at regular time in hospital canteen. Now my stomach already has problems due to irregular operations and irregular eating time. A medical doctor in traditional Chinese medicine hardly has any operation, if they occasionally have an operation, they can arrange time of operation easily."

Clearly, this is an insider's account for the traditional Chinese medicine from several interesting, but very practical angles, which reflect what the Chinese think.

Personally, I do not consider that the traditional Chinese medicine would have a great development although many people are still studying it simply because we cannot get the insight created by ancient great geniuses from a theory without clear cut-off line, we cannot advance a science when we do not have the talent that ancient great geniuses had.

This argument is similar to the facts that few scientists can advance the Newton theory a lot within Newton's frame, few scientists can advance the Euclidean geometry a lot within Euclidean frame, etc., simply we do not have the talents that Newton and Euclid had.

Before ending this section, let me restate the conversation on which specialty is the best in Western medicine, which again reflects what the Chinese think.

I asked: "Which specialty is the best in Western medicine?"

"Dentist!" :she/he answered.

"Why?"

"Because each person has 32 teeth, so a dentist will never loss her/his job. By clear contrast, each person has only one appendix, so a surgeon will have nothing to do after taking out the appendix from a patient, but a dentist will always have a lot of work to do, because no patient will take out all her/his 32 teeth in a single visit to a dentist. Even a dentist has taken all 32 teeth out from a patient, she/he still has the job to install 32 false teeth, but a surgeon cannot install an artificial appendix in a patient!"

4.1.3 Other Theories

In fact, most so-called Chinese theories were obtained from subjectively metal meditation without objectively scientific observation and validation, as the Chinese sage says [25]: "got knowledge without traveling". Such theories would be crashed heavily with the reality, because even the sages cannot predict the future, and thus their applications were limited.

Actually I am quite disappointed by the Chinese ability to create a systematical theory, we, Chinese, have the longest feudalism, but our scholars in social sciences cannot write several detailed studies on Chinese feudalism at world level if they cannot write the detailed analysis on Chinese socialism.

Also they could not write series of books on feudal economy, which should be the best topic to write. Actually a British wrote the best book on Chinese scientific and technological history [37], while the Chinese are busy discussing how an important role Needham's Chinese wife played in writing these books.

All these suggest that the Chinese still live in the time, when a single sentence can be the truth, but now we know that a single sentence represents a single aspect of truth. This is the limitation of human language and thinking as said in The Lost World [38]: "the human brain cannot think of two things simultaneously."

4.2 Scientific Observation

In Chinese language, we have no clear distinction between accuracy and precision, my personal understanding is the accuracy is the real number that an object has but the precision is the number that we measure, therefore I really do not know exactly if the Chinese history is reliably documented.

A historical case, which is frequently praised by various Chinese as a model of exact record of history, is as follows [11]. There was a big problem between Duke Ling of Jin and his prime minister, Zhao Dun. The Duke Ling of Jin decided to take a chance to kill Zhao in his palace, but the plot fell and Zhao ran away from the palace. Zhan Dun's nephew, General Zhao Chuan, told Zhao Dun not to go out the kingdom, but to wait for his news to decide if Zhao Dun needed to run away. Some days after that, General Zhao Chuan's soldiers killed Duke Ling of Jin in Park Peach, so Zhao Dun came back safely to his power. Afterwards, Zhao Dun one day found that the officer, who was responsible for recording the history, wrote that Zhao Dun killed the Duke Ling of Jin in Park Peach. Zhao Dun argued that he was then about 100 km from the Park Peach, how could he kill the Duke? The officer answered that he should have planed this plot otherwise he should condemn and kill General Zhao Chuan after Zhao Dun regained his power if he did not know this plot. In my view this is not exactly accurate and precise history but the deduction of historical facts, because even Zhao Dun plotted to kill Duke Ling of Jin, the fact is that he did not kill Duke Ling of Jin in person.

Perhaps, the Chinese are not good at numbers, as Lao Tzu (Tsu) says [25]: “The Tao produced One; One produced Two; Two produced Three; Three produced All things.” This statement is very similar to the narrative made by Gamow [39]: “There is a story two Hungarian aristocrats who decided to play a game in which the one who calls the largest number wins. ‘Well,’ said one of them, ‘you name your number first.’ After a few minutes of hard mental work the second aristocrat finally named the largest number he could think of. ‘Three,’ he said. Now it was the turn of the first one to do the thinking, but after a quarter of an hour he finally gave up. . . . We have it indeed on the authority of African explorers that many Hottentot tribes do not have in their vocabulary the names of for numbers larger than three. Ask a native down there how many sons he has or how many enemies he has slain, and if the number is more than three he will answer ‘many’.”

The current knowledge on the birth of Lao Tzu (Tsu) could be dated to 600 BC and the earliest version of The Tao Teh King could be dated between 202 BC and 8 AD. Then the ancient Chinese sage is not used to name the number larger than three, of course though he might have more deep insight in his statement.

On the one hand, China might lack great thinkers, on the other hand, the lack of accurate and precise documentations made a great difficulty for Chinese scholars to build up a systematical theory.

An important difference between modern and ancient sciences is the scientific observation, without which we cannot have the detailed records on the processes of natural and social phenomena.

As the Chinese science lagged behind the rest world far away, the Chinese are generally not good at scientific observation, which should include the details and quantifying.

In general, the Chinese are good at literature styled description but are not good at technical and uninteresting details. In other words, besides literature, it is hard for the Chinese people to study something in great details, while currently people generally consider that a small detail can decide the fate of a big event [40, 41].

Without details, one could fill the vacuum only with imaginations. This is particularly visible in Chinese classical literature, where one can frequently find such a sentence as this fact can be proved or witnessed by the following poem. That is to say that the Chinese people use poems as a hard and solid historical evidence to verify a historical fact, which leads the difficulty to distinguish which is the really historical record and which is the legend. Although it is said that the history is written by victors [42], the reality is that the history is something, which can be modified randomly and purposely for making money worldwide.

The scientific observation is directly related to the observation in daily life. For example, the Russian army parades have been televised in China many times, during which the presenters with a Russian language scholar talked and commented the parades. Although they noticed the difference in goose-step between Chinese and Russian armies, they did not detail these differences such as that the Russians use their left hand to hold the rifle, while the Chinese use their right hand to hold the rifle.

Without details, every measure issued by government could become to the empty words and slogan. Thus, even at the best intention, many measures have been overdone in Chinese history. The recent example would be the culture revolution from 1966 to 1976, for which many people blamed Mao Zedong, however I would arguably suggest that there are many damages due to overdoing because our Chinese are not used to give many details, therefore the exercise of various measures would have many different versions according to the people who exercised.

4.3 Logic

The Chinese language is a language very different from other languages not only in view of difficulty, but more important is that a foreign word is very difficult to penetrate into the Chinese language as a Chinese word to survive. In general, Chinese scholars always try to find the meaning of a foreign word to translate this foreign word into a Chinese word, even try to find the meanings from chemical words.

If there would be no word with similar meaning in Chinese language, Chinese scholars would create a Chinese word with the same or similar meaning of foreign word without similarity in foreign pronunciation. This phenomenon is more evident in scientific terms, and philosophical terms, for example, metaphysics.

It is only the time when Chinese scholars cannot find a similar meaning word in Chinese language, and cannot create a Chinese word with the same or similar meaning, and then they directly create a Chinese word with the foreign pronunciation without explaining the meaning of this new created word, especially the word related to abstractive meaning. Although the Chinese language has a trend to use foreign words as fashionable way recently, the Chinese language is very strongly immune to the penetration of foreign words.

In this sense, the logic is the word, which is directly adopted in Chinese language with the same pronunciation without explaining its meaning. This means that the Chinese scholars could not find a Chinese word with a similar meaning in Chinese language when they first met this word.

In reality, the Chinese indeed lack logic. That is to say that the Chinese have difficulty to determine the logic order of a sequence of events. This is possible because there is no tense in Chinese language, and the Chinese language uses adverbs to determine what happened in the past, what is happening now and what will happen in the future. Needless to say, there is also no past perfect, future perfect, and so on in Chinese language. As a result the Chinese oral language is one of easiest languages to learn in world [3].

The lack of logic would lead the Chinese people frequently to have a completely different view from westerners, also the Chinese people frequently mix the cause and consequence reversibly, this is by no means of intention, but is simply due to the different Chinese logic structure.

For example, a Chinese PhD once told me that the reason of rise and fall of departments in several universities, where she/he studied and worked, is due to her/his present and absence. The logic in this statement is: (i) the cause is her/his present and absence and (ii) the consequence is the rise and fall of departments. In my view, the real facts and logic sequence should be: she/he had the opportunity to study or work in those departments because the departments went up and had money, and she/he had to leave because the departments fell and had no more money to support her/him.

Before US presidential election in 2008, a book was published in Chinese, Obama, who changed the US, or literally Changed US's Obama [43]. The logic sequence of this title is quite confusing in my view, say, who changed which or which changed whom, (i) Obama changed the US, which we have yet to see, because Obama had yet to be elected at that time, or (ii) the US changed Obama, who grows up there as a black, or (iii) the US people changed Obama because they would vote for him. However, the latter two explanations of book title are opposite to the meaning of this Chinese book.

The medical doctor in traditional Chinese medicine uses four techniques to make a diagnosis: watching, smelling, asking, and touching. The touching mainly means the measurement of pulses, however, this term, measurement of pulses (ba mai), is often used in various circumstances. For example, the Chinese journalists often report some well-known experts "measured the pulses of Chinese stock markets for next year". This again is a logic mistake, because the measurement of pulses is to measure the current situation to make a diagnosis on the past rather than to make a prognosis in future.

Very similar to the case of adoption of word, logic, into Chinese language, the word, geometry, also directly penetrated into Chinese language with foreign pronunciation but unclear meaning. The only possible explanation is that the Chinese are not good at space and measurement, which was acknowledged by a Chinese scholar that there was no exact measurement on land unit, mu, in Chinese history [44]. Actually the Euclidian geometry is a very logic deduction. If the Chinese are not good at logic, then naturally they are not good at Euclidian geometry, which is not an easy subject for Chinese students once.

The consequence of lack of logic is the confusion of original with derivative, and confusion of major point with minor point. For example, once I met a friend who got an MS degree in English literature. She/he told me that she/he was busy translating the Russian writer, Ivan Sergeevich Turgenev's novel, Rudin, from English version to Chinese. I suggested to her/his that Rudin was already published in Chinese language many years ago. However, she/he told me that the previous Chinese version translated directly from Russian language has many mistakes, which she/he did not provide any evidence to prove, so she/he now was retranslating this book from English version in order to correct these mistakes although she/he completely does not know Russian language. In my view, this is the confusion of original with derivative, because all the correctness of translations should be based on the original language, the Russian language rather than other translated versions.

In 2005, I visited a historical site, Pool Hua Qing, Xi'an, province Shannxi, where the famous Xi'an incident occurred, then Generals Chang Hsueh-liang and Yang Hucheng arrested Generalissimo Chiang Kai-shek to ask him to defend China against Japanese invasion. The tourist guide working in Pool Hua Qing told visitors how great Chiang Kai-shek was because he did not smoke and did not drink alcohol. I really wonder how we can evaluate a leader based on her/his personal behavior rather than her/his leadership.

In fact, there is no clause in Chinese language to further define the meaning of preceding word, and the lack of clause could be one of many reasons why the Chinese people lack accuracy and precision.

Actually the lack of accuracy, precision, and logic can be found in other nationals, for example, Mr. Snow in his White House press briefing on the Saddam's verdict in January 4, 2007 said [45]: "And the point I made yesterday is that there is -- at least among the American press, the fascination with the final moments and the relatively less description of the first 69 years." This is not accurate and precise because it is hard to think that Saddam did anything against humanity before he was 10-year old.

The implication is that each national has the possibility to make logic mistakes unconsciously.

Chapter 5

CHINESE WAR

As far as I remember, at the late stage of culture revolution (1966-1976) in China, a newspaper, Inner Reference, which then had a limited circulation, began to publish a series of small articles called Today in History. This is perhaps the first time for our generation to know this type of articles on history. Of course this series of Today in History were translated from English, therefore it has more contents on the UK history than on the history of other countries.

Currently there are many different versions of Today in History available, but I already have no time to read them, thus my impression on Today in History is mainly biased on the version that I read in the newspaper many years ago. Based on that version, it seems that there is war in each calendar day in UK history. However, most wars are not civil wars, and these wars are generally not conducted in UK soil, but in the soils of other countries.

What I discussed in the previous two chapters is in fact related to the first of three ways, by which a country can become a world power, namely, the production or application of systematical theory on distribution of social wealth and exercise of social justice. The second way is what we read in UK history. This is to say the world entitlement. It means that the regional and world entitlement is largely accomplished by means of military power. This suggests that we need to examine the Chinese wars in history in order to find the long-term trend if the Chinese can use this approach to becoming a world power.

If we look at the Chinese history, we can find that most wars were conducted inside China, in Chinese soil. There are indeed many wars in Chinese history, however most wars are related to the overthrowing of previous reign. In fact, these wars are civil wars. There is almost no war in Chinese history related to colonization of other countries and expansion of border. Perhaps, the only formal war related to the regional entitlement is the Korean War during 50s of last century.

There are indeed wars in Chinese history for defending of motherland, but the final aim is generally limited to expel the foreign invaders out of Chinese borders rather than to furthermore conduct the wars into foreign country to overthrow the government of invaders, and establish a puppet government serving for benefit of China. With respect to the previous chapters, I would suggest that a national would not defend herself, if she could not defend any principle.

In this sense, most wars in Chinese history play the role of transforming the social wealth from old regime to new regime with little advance of social life because a new regime generally uses the old social systems, too.

5.1 Religious War

Naturally, the above comparison is only related to the location, where the war is conducted. I would suggest that the religious wars account for a large part of wars in human history. Even sometimes some people consider that the war on terror is a new religious war as initially referenced by President Bush as a "crusade" against terrorism [46].

When we look back the Chinese history, we can find that there is almost no formally religious war in China although some people might argue the religious conflicts occurred sometimes in China. The religious war perhaps is the best way to demonstrate if a national really has a belief, for which a national can sacrifice herself. In the previous chapter, I suggested that any religion in China is simply a show and a luxurious business but not a serious belief, the fact, which the religious wars were never conducted in Chinese history, would serve as a further proof for my argument.

In this view, the Chinese as a national never made a serious decision to sacrifice this nation for any religious belief although some scholars would suggest that the Taiping rebellion could be considered as a somewhat religious war [47]. This is not the real fact in my view. The new religion was only an excuse for the beginning of Taiping Heavenly Kingdom, under this religious cover, and the war was going against the non-Han government. This is so, because almost all the policies applied by Taiping Heavenly Kingdom government are still Chinese traditional ones without any significant difference with respect to religious belief.

The really religious war is not a war for any personal interests, at least on the surface the people would say so. For example, French Wars of Religion, the problem as presented by Alexandre Dumas in The Three Musketeers [48]: ". . ., who have committed no other crime than singing in French the psalms we sing in Latin?" Clearly, the Chinese never have such a problem on whether you read your prayers in mandarin or any other local Chinese dialect, even the Chinese never dream to declare a war for this reason.

The implication for anyone would be that it is very hard, even practically impossible, to overthrow any Chinese government under the name of a religion although many non-Chinese dream so. This is so because the first aim of religion in China is just a luxurious business to show that we are rich and how we can spend our money randomly. The second aim of religion serves for extreme practical aim in daily-life.

The people with extremely practical and concrete aim in daily-life are afraid of sacrificing their life for a highly abstract religion.

Therefore there is no religious war in Chinese history, the Chinese would not sacrifice them for any religion in the form of a national war, either civil war or war with other countries, because the Chinese indeed do not bother themselves with the issue of religions. This is the long-term trend for Chinese in this regard.

5.2 Colonization, Resource and Market War

The human history suggests that the wars for colonization would account for a considerable amount of wars, however I would suggest that the Chinese are highly unlikely to conduct any serious war with the pure aim to colonize other nationals.

In fact, the word, colonization, is not considered as a word with neutral or any positive meaning in Chinese language, but a word with purely negative meaning in modern Chinese language. When other nationals talk about the colonization of Moon or Mars, the Chinese can only talk about the exploration of Moon or Mars, because the colonization is not a positive word, which goes against Chinese moral.

It is said that the UK had no ability to confront the powers in European continent, thus she extended her influence to the other continents. If so, this means that the colonization war is conducted by powerful country against small and weak countries. This concept is frequently denounced by ancient Chinese sages, thus the Chinese have little willing to conduct such a war, although in Chinese history there are many wars conducted in a pattern that the big kingdom conquers small kingdoms, which are conducted under name of unifying China.

Another type of war, which is directly related to existence of a national, is the resource war, for example, the potential war between Israel and Syria for the water resource, the potential war between Egypt and countries located in upstream of Nile. This type of war does not exist in Chinese history at all, simply because China has vast resources in the past, which are far sufficient for feudally stable economy in China.

The war for marketing, for example, two opium wars led by the UK on China to open Chinese markets. This type of war also does not exist in Chinese history simply because China did not have a vast production ability in her history.

5.3 CHARACTERISTICS OF CHINESE WAR

As the Chinese army has few chances to be involved in religious, colonization, resource and market wars, the Chinese army in long-term trend is an internal-oriented army rather than an external-oriented army, which is similar to the situations in most Asian countries, for example, the army in Thailand concentrates around her capital for the need of swift coup d'état. This is the big difference between Chinese and western power armies.

Therefore before the foreign military coachers came to China, perhaps the only way to get the original ideas on combat is the religious war and resistant war against foreign invaders, because these combats would be governed by different thoughts on strategy and tactics. As there are almost no religious war and fewer resistant wars in Chinese history, this means that the Chinese army traditionally conducts wars inside Chinese soil within the same frame passed by generations from ancient Chinese sages such as Sun Tzu [49], who defines the doctrine of war.

The war with same doctrines, language, technique, equipments, spying, communications, and other related issues makes the war become anything in a closed system without power of novelty and vitality. By clear contrast, the military combats in western power represent the most advanced idea, concept, strategy, tactics, technique and equipments. Therefore the Chinese army stayed with cold weapons for thousands of years, and applied the oldest military idea and strategy from Sun Tzu's time to real combats.

Consequently, for a long time, the war in Chinese history becomes a somewhat personal activity or the competition in Chinese martial arts between two generals no mater how many soldiers involved in combat, as we read in classical Chinese novels [11, 31, 50], where the result of concrete battle depended on kung fu of two generals, which can be predetermined. The battle became a sport game rather than collective efforts. Perhaps, this is one reason why Chinese martial arts are still so popular and advocated in nuclear era, which can be seen in Hollywood films, where white people use helicopters, black people use guns, and Chinese people use kung fu, naturally, the kung fu can beat helicopters and guns in money-making films, but the Chinese history tell us that the kung fu cannot defend this country for quite a long time.

On the other hand, this type of war leaves few reliable records on the details of war and how to conduct the war. Thus one has difficulty to determine if the details come from fiction novels or from real records. We, as Chinese ourselves, do not know, for example, the exact number and composition of Chinese troop in ancient time in each battle, this is a very clear contrast to what we read in the book related to Roman Empire, where we can read [51]: "The constitution of the Imperial legion may be described in a few words. The heavy-armed infantry, which composed its principle strength, was divided into ten cohorts, and fifty-five companies, under the orders of a correspondent number of tribunes and centurions. The first cohort, which always claimed the post of honor and the custody of the eagle, was formed of eleven hundred and five soldiers, the most approved for valor and fidelity. . ".

The poor records and imaginations in Chinese history make Chinese generals have little chance to simulate or remodel or reconstruct any real battle scientifically in Chinese history, and are not used to analyze the battles in human history in numeric sense. This is again different from European power, for example, the Soviet Marshall Georgy Zhukov mentioned that he had simulated quite a lot of battles in World War I during his time in Belarus [52]. These simulations are almost impossible for Chinese generals because it is really hard to find the detailed records on the battles in Chinese history. The only consequence is that Chinese generals could not advance the Chinese military theory too much.

Practically it is very hard for Chinese troop to go beyond Chinese language barrier although there are indeed several wars beyond Chinese border. An important aspect in the wars conducted according to Chinese doctrines passed from ancient sages is to get the mind of enemies, thus the Chinese generally do not conduct the war against small and weak countries, this is a clear contract to western powers, even in the case the war had to be conducted in enemy land, the Chinese troop generally withdraws after victory (not conquest) in order to get the mind of people.

Hence, the wars in Chinese history play the role in transferring the social wealth and destroying the environments as we read how fire destroyed 125-km long palaces in dynasty Qin, do not change the Chinese thinking system too much and do not create a new social system.

In fact, the wars conducted in Chinese history are very costly, not only in terms of life, but also in terms of money. I would suggest this type of war totally against the cost-effective. Such poorly cost-effective war can be read from the following [24]: "The long and splendid reign of Emperor K'ang His, lasting from

1662 until 1723, made his name more celebrated than that of any other Asiatic monarch. Yet it was in the reign of this greatest of Chinese rulers that the Chinese patriotic pirate, known under the name of Koxinga, ravaged the coasts of the provinces of Kuangtung and Fukien to such a degree that the government junks were totally unable to cope with him. Under these circumstances, K'ang His hit upon the happy expedient of ordering all the people inhabiting this extended coast line to retire into the interior to a distance of thirty li, or about nine miles, at which point they were inaccessible even to such stout attacks as this adherent of the old order of things was able to make. This strange command was generally obeyed, and was quite successful . . . Every foreigner reading this singular account is impelled to assent to the comment of the author of the 'Middle Kingdom,' that a government which was strong enough to compel such a number of maritime subjects to leave their towns and villages, and to retire at such great loss into the interior, ought to have been strong enough to equip a fleet and to put an end to the attacks upon these desolated homes."

Chapter 6

LAST APPROACH

If the long-term trend in Chinese history suggests that the Chinese have little chance to rely on their army, which is internal-oriented and poorly cost-effective, to execute the world entitlement, the becoming of a world power by means of entitlement would be unlikely to be suitable for Chinese. Even many Chinese have the intention or dream to use the military might as an approach to make China become a world power, the cost-effectiveness would go strongly against this possibility.

The humans have advanced to such a stage, which seems to me that the world entitlement is going more and more against the cost-effective. Let us look at the cost-effective in ancient wars as Dumas described the war in his novel [53]:

"I believe I have read in Plutarch that Alexander the Great, when he started for India, took with him but eighteen or twenty talents in gold, something like one hundred or one hundred and twenty thousand francs. Now, do you suppose that with these eighteen or twenty talents alone he fed his army, won the battle of Granicus, subdued Asia Minor, conquered Tyre, Gaza, Syria and Egypt, built Alexandria, penetrated to Lybia, had himself declared Son of Jupiter by the oracle of Ammon, penetrated as far as the Hyphases, and, when his soldiers refused to follow him further, returned to Babylon, where he surpassed in luxury, debauchery and self-indulgence the most debauched and voluptuous of the kings of Asia? Did Macedonia furnish his supplies? Do you believe that King Philip, most indigent of the kings of poverty-stricken Greece, honored the drafts his son drew upon him? Not so. Alexander . . . pillaged cities, held kings for ransom, levied contributions from the conquered countries. Let us turn to Hannibal. You know how he left Carthage, don't you? He did not have even the eighteen or twenty talents of his predecessor; and as he needed money, he seized and sacked the city of Saguntum in the midst of peace, in defiance of the fealty of treaties. After that he was rich and could begin his campaign. Forgive me if this time I no longer quote Plutarch, but Cornelius Nepos. I will spare you the details of his descent from the Pyrenees, how he crossed the Alps and the three battles which he won, seizing each time the treasures of the vanquished, and turn to the five or six years he spent in Campania. Do you believe that he and his army paid the Capuans for their subsistence, and that the bankers of Carthage, with whom he had quarrelled, supplied him with funds? No; war fed war . . . Let us pass on to Cæsar. Ah, Cæsar! That's another story. He left for Spain with some thirty millions of debt, and returned with practically the same. He started for Gaul, where he spent ten years with our ancestors. During these ten years he sent over one hundred millions to Rome, repassed the Alps, crossed the Rubicon, marched straight to the Capitol, forced the gates of the Temple of Saturn, where the treasury was, seized sufficient for his private needs--and not for those of the Republic--three thousand pounds of gold in ingots; and died (he whom creditors twenty years earlier refused to allow to leave his little house in the Suburra) leaving two or three thousand sesterces per head to the citizens, ten or twelve millions to Calpurnia, and thirty or forty millions to Octavius."

"War feeds war", this statement is not fully valid according to the current moral standard. Thus, a country that assumes a world entitlement could be backfired, that is, the high cost of modern war could lead a country to bankruptcy or the change of governments, which is so-called the stable or unstable dilemma in Chinese history.

In fact, there are no more treasures such as gold, silver, and gems, which can be got in a war when conquering a city, because almost anything else in modern society is either bought using credit card or loaned from bank.

Until this point, among the three approaches to becoming a would power, the Chinese are highly unlikely to have the first two, i.e. the production of systematical theory on distribution of social wealth and exercise of social justice, and the regional and world entitlement, then the only approach remained is the opportunity.

6.1 Stable and Unstable

Many Chinese scholars have indicated that the Chinese society is a super-stable system, which seems to be true, because (i) each reign in Chinese history did her best to maintain the stability of Chinese society, (ii) the Chinese have the longest period of feudalism in the world, and (iii) the Chinese society is quiet and peaceful in most of time of history.

However, I would argue that there are far more dynasties in Chinese history than in the history of all other countries. This suggests that the rise and fall of dynasties occur far more frequently in China than in other countries, namely, there are far much more revolutions or rebellions in Chinese history, which result in the overthrowing of old dynasties and building of new dynasties or rebuilding of old social system and structure.

In such a case, the Chinese society is a super-unstable system, or the Chinese society is a super-stable system in short-term, but a super-unstable system in long-term. This again is the dilemma in Chinese history.

This short-term super-stable is due to the fact that each reign in Chinese history created a short-term stability, but also created a long-term instability, because the problems generated in short-term stability would be accumulated without solutions and notices.

As a self-reliance country without modern technology in the past, the stable was more related to stable life and a feudally stale economy because the frequently peasant revolutions in Chinese history did not bring any new social system, that is, China was still a self-reliance country. The stability was heavily dependent on the natural condition, mainly weather.

On the other hand, the unstable in Chinese history suggested the massive destruction of wealth accumulated by previous dynasties. This is so, because the Chinese have no particular concept that the wealth belong to Chinese people as a whole, but regarded the wealth as the symbols of dynasties to destroy as said by Giles [3]: "Patriotism is quite unknown to the Chinese." In fact, I really wonder what the patriotism means for Chinese, because a Chinese professor once said that the buying of apartment is patriotism when the house market began to decline.

This is somewhat different from part of western reasoning, for example, some protesters wanted to set fire on the building of parliamentary during 5th October revolution in the Federal Republic of Yugoslavia, but they were persuaded to abandon this idea because the parliamentary building belongs to Serbia people, not Slobodan Milosevic.

In this sense, China indeed needs stable. With current sciences and technology, the stability is related to the development. However, the dilemma is that the China's market and resource are mainly located outside of China, and the new ideas and concepts come in with other raw materials. For China's market and resource, China could assume the world entitlement, however China has no ability or tradition to use the regional or world entitlements to become a world power.

Actually I would suggest the stability and instability at world level, because this is the condition, which could provide the opportunity for China to become a world power. In this context, I would suggest that all the world powers hope the stability, because this is the way to maintain their dominant positions. This simply means that all international organizations were created to maintain the world stability, which is the hope of all the world powers. This is why Japan, as a new emerging power before World War II, rejected the request made by League of Nations.

From viewpoint of rise and fall of international organization, World War II only played a role to change from League of Nations to United Nations, but such a change costs so many lives.

Frankly speaking, I would strongly suggest that China needs a stable world, which is identical with the hope of current world powers, because China still holds important positions in international organizations built from scratch of World War II, and benefits from them.

6.2 Lag Time and Validation

The traditional Chinese system is not a fast reactive system because the Chinese people are not very sensitive to the events occurred beyond their immediately direct interests and cannot make an instant decision. Therefore, there is always a lag time between Chinese and western thoughts, and between what is popular in outside world and what is popular inside China, although there is a lag time in thoughts among different levels of Chinese; between developed and underdeveloped regions, etc., which are beyond the scope of this book.

The lag time, on one side, is due to the difficulty in translation between foreign and Chinese languages, on the other side, is partially due to the copyright law, which leads the massive translation of works not under the protection of copyright law, however these books are generally out-of-date. Of course, this is by no means that China should abolish the international copyright laws.

The advance of technology makes the information propagate more easily than ever before, namely, the information as gravity can feel instantly. However, the Chinese have to use time to absorb and digest the new information and concept, on the other hand, the ability of absorption and digestion of new ideas in humans does not evolve much to keep the pace of advance of technology.

The web 2.0 makes the information stratified according to different groups of interests, where people gather, thus the information seems to be more difficult to penetrate through the barriers between groups, thus I would suggest that the lag time between Chinese and western thoughts would be likely to increase because western thoughts would be buried by popularly luxurious thoughts, and the taste of Chinese people have the trend forwards to the things occurred around themselves with respect to eating, drinking, playing and enjoying pleasure.

The lag time between China and the rest of world suggests that the Chinese live in somewhat older time, if not ancient time in this sense. For example, in China the most popular gesture before photo camera is to put two figures to be "V", which is the gesture, as said, used by the US army during the World War II. In fact this gesture is still somewhat popular in Japan. However we cannot find the president Bush using such a gesture if we look at the TV footage.

Another example related to the lag time can be evidence by what is currently broadcasted by Hong Kong radio, which spends hundreds of hours to broadcast the Chinese songs popular in 30s of 20th century and American songs popular in 60s of 20th century. And even one presenter claimed that the best songs in the world are the songs in the US in 60s of 20th century.

The lag time suggests that the Chinese are very unlikely to be able to take the advantage from the opportunity presented before them in history, even could not see the opportunity with their out-of-date knowledge.

In modern world, the validation could become more and more important, because the current technology makes the spread of new ideas very easily.

As scientific thoughts began in China very late, the Chinese lack the ability of validation of any thoughts coming from abroad. The validation of thoughts coming from abroad is unthinkable for Chinese, because the Chinese are used to either accept all the ideas without objection or to completely reject all the ideas without reasoning. Therefore China becomes a laboratory of second-hand ideas, concepts and thoughts, which in principle could not give a light of incoming opportunity in front of Chinese.

The lack of validation again presents another danger for Chinese to take the advantage from an opportunity because the invalidated ideas could explain the opportunity from the view, which is not benefit for Chinese.

Both lead to the dilemma for Chinese in taking the advantage from an opportunity.

6.3 Generation Dynamics and Kinetics

The generation dynamics should be the behaviors of a generation of Chinese, while the generation kinetics should be the motivations of a generation of Chinese.

Actually, the generation dynamics can include behaviors, fashions, what people read, watch, play, clothes, even diseases, etc., or as the Chinese commonly say: clothing, eating, housing and traveling. In other words, the generation dynamics should be something on the surface, which is easily visible.

In this sense, the generation kinetics can include motivations, aims, goals, what people think, pursue, dream, like, dislike, love, etc. In other words, the generation kinetics should be something inside human mind, which is not visible.

The problem raised here is whether the generation dynamics and kinetics can pass from generation to generation. If this process can continue, that is, the dynamics and kinetics between generations are the same, and then we would expect to see a stable country and a stable world. If the difference in dynamics and kinetics between generations would be too large to be tolerant then the crash between generations would lead to the traditional Chinese revolutions or rebellions.

In the ancient China, we would say the dynamics and kinetics could easily pass from generation to generation, because there is almost no change in social and environmental surroundings. Then the only difference between generations could be the different dynasties, but the memory for the previous dynasty would vanish within two generations as read in classical Chinese novel Three Kingdoms [50].

Certainly, external forces, either the advance of science and technology or foreign invasions, change the generation dynamics and kinetics, especially in China. For example, the opium war significantly changed the Chinese generation dynamics and kinetics, because it leads to the overthrow of the last dynasty in China eventually. On the other hand, the advance of science and technology changes the generation dynamics and kinetics without a drop of blood.

Thus, what is the Chinese generation dynamics in short-term and long-term? The Chinese history suggests that the long-term trend in generation dynamics is very simple: eating, drinking, playing and enjoying pleasure within the limited space behind the Great Wall. The short-term trend in generation dynamics is also very simple: as a national without belief, this national has to use the belief from other nationals. When an imported belief fails, the national belief would return to the original needs in life, which are the long-term trend for Chinese, eating, drinking, playing and enjoying pleasure.

The long-term generation kinetics is similarly very simple for ordinary Chinese, which is money because the Chinese history shows such a trend over years and the current Chinese generation kinetics goes along this long-term trend for this and next generations at least. For the educated Chinese, the long-term purchase of female ornaments, the wealth of the state was irrecoverable given away to foreign and hostile nations." Likely this is a long-term trend for all nationals, not especially for Chinese, that is, the men with their ideas and images are the focus of a country during the wartime, but the women with their ideas and images are the focus of a country during the peaceful time.

In fact, there are many women, who pretend men to serve in army in Chinese history, which leads Mao Zedong's poem [55], Militia Women: How bright and brave they look / shouldering five-foot rifles on the parade ground lit up by the first gleams of day / China's daughters have high-aspiring minds / They love their battle array, not silks and satins.

Moreover, China officially abolished the polygyny not long before, the fact that many women in a family would lead to men to be less aggressive, need-to-be-cared and family-oriented, simply because the focus of women is different from that of men, still because children are likely to spend more time with their mother and listen to their mother, and the Chinese men generally have no ideas on what to do.

The feminization in peaceful time is the long-term trend for Chinese men, whose focus is woman, love and money. Actually we can see far more images related to women in Chinese society than related to men. The following popular song could serve as an example of feminization: "I have not been able to see your femininity again, I lonely row that small boat, I have not been able to grasp your small hands, let tears flood in my mind, . . . is this because I am not femininity enough so you planed to leave without looking at me . . ." This is so perhaps because [56] "I will tell you that women like such timidity . . ."

7.2 Rich Imagination

The creation of Chinese written language is really amazing, because it is extremely hard to imagine that such ideography can represent human ideas, especially very abstract concepts, without any connection with pronunciation. By clear contrast, the alphabet system is quite simple, because the only need in this system is to reliably record what people pronounce.

Thus I would suggest that the Chinese people are full of imagination, which can also be evidenced by the classical Chinese novel, Journey to the West [29], and huge numbers of poems in Chinese history. In Chinese classical novels and real life, the Chinese people frequently praise someone, who can read something not written in the book or something behind the text, for example, General Sun Quan, one of three warlords in Chinese classical novel Three Kingdoms [50]. I would suggest that something not written in the book or behind the text is either imagination or implication, but more likely to be imagination because the implication would be related to the text.

Another extremely famous anecdote in Chinese history is related to two greatest Chinese sages, Lao Tzu and Confucius. One day, Confucius with his students visited Lao Tzu, who sat silently in the room, with the purpose of asking some questions or discussing some issues. After waiting a long time, Lao Tzu opened his mouth, and asked Confucius if his teeth were still in his mouth. "No." :answered Confucius. Then Lao Tzu asked: "Is my tongue in my mouth?" "Yes." :Confucius answered. Then Confucius left the room with his students because the visit was finished. A student asked Confucius that we had not yet ask Lao Tzu any question. Confucius answered that Lao Tzu had already taught us a lot, that is, the soft can beat the hard, which is the meaning drawn from the fact that there are no more teeth in Lao Tzu's mouth, but there is still the tongue in Lao Tzu's mouth, while the teeth are hard and the tongue is soft. This anecdote gets tons of praises on these two Chinese sages throughout Chinese history. However I would suggest that this anecdote is the pure imagination either from Confucius or from the people living after Confucius.

Still, this so-called great philosophy, which the soft wins the hard, is not philosophical at all, because the really hard fact is that the teeth can cut the tongue into pieces. By this philosophy, China lost the war, which could win under other philosophies, for example, the Sino-French War [57]. Under other philosophies, Japanese declared the war, which has completely no hope to win, for example, World War II; while Americans conduct the wars, which can be won easily, or let others fight for Americans when the war cannot be won, such as Vietnams War.

Consequently, I would argue that the Chinese philosophy is built upon the soft imagination rather than the hard facts. I would also suggest that the imagination goes mostly along the Chinese written language rather than other concrete subjects, for example, the Chinese calligraphy is the art going around the Chinese written language. For another example on this topic, anyone arrives at China during the period of Chinese New Year, she/he would easily notice that there is a piece of paper stuck on the door of Chinese family. The Chinese character written on it is Blessing/Good Fortune, however this Chinese character was stuck upside-down in many families. This is to say that this Chinese character is 180 degrees reversed from the same character printed in books. So is done because the pronunciation of upside-down is similar to the pronunciation of arrival in Chinese, thus the imaginable explanation for upside-down Blessing/Good Fortune is the arrival of Blessing/Good Fortune.

A national is good at imagination, would be weak at scientific observation, because the scientific observation is generally uninteresting and monotonous without any beautiful imagination. However, it is the scientific observation that constructs the base for any serious systematical thoughts related to mankind, it is only scientific observation can create the detailed records rather than fiction-styled Chinese history such as Popular Romances on Chinese History [58]. Without scientific observation, one cannot perform any scientific experiments, which are the foundation for modern science and technology. Therefore, the Chinese spend more time to analyze a personal characteristic rather than to spend time to analyze the natural phenomena.

Again, the Chinese names could be a great thing of imagination, which are not similar to the European names in disposal and anyone can take a name from the existing names, but the Chinese need to take pains and troubles to think out a name unique, not only being unique from other people's names, but also being good from views of geomantic omen, religion, etc.

Yet, a national is good at imagination, would be weak at action, because it usually takes a long time for Chinese to react, and everything has the possibility of becoming empty words without concrete action, which in some sense is consistent with what Chinese sage says [25]: "Therefore the sage, in the exercise of his government, empties their minds, fills their bellies, weakens their wills, and strengthens their bones. He constantly tries to keep them without knowledge and without desire, and where there are those who have knowledge, to keep them from presuming to act on it. When there is this abstinence from action, good order is universal." This is what Theodore Roosevelt said [59]: ". . . the Chinese had constructed an inefficient governmental system based in part on the theory of written competitive examinations."

Moreover, a national is good at imagination, would be strong in production of rumors and would be more interested in rumors, because most rumors are based on imaginations rather than any hard facts or little fact besides the rumors that are deliberately made. For example, I was told that Zhang Fei, a hero and General in classical Chinese novel Three Kingdoms [50], was in fact a pretty much polite and exquisite person, but Guan Yu, another hero and General in the same novel, is a very rude person. This is a contradiction to what describes in the novel on the one hand. On the other hand, I really wonder where she/he got this fact, because these people lived in 2 000 years ago, and currently no reliable record is available on the characteristics of these two persons. This is certainly an imagination.

The direct result is that the Chinese have the trend to study soft-science rather than hard-science, consequently, more Chinese favor the way to be an official rather than to be an entrepreneur, because at least partly the imagination required theories would be revised in other countries as we have seen in history in USSR and China.

On the other hand, although the US is the dreamland for many people, it is also unlikely to see any new thoughts coming from the US on distribution of social wealth and exercise of social justice. However, the Americans and British are more likely to produce systematical theories on economics.

The Chinese history does not provide any convincing evidence that the Chinese can create any systematical theory related to the distribution of social wealth and exercise of social justice within Chinese soil. Therefore the new systematical theory is unlikely to be born in China in future. However, China currently follows the Marxism, which is mainly focused on the studies on capitalism, even how to destroy the capitalism with respect to the Leninism and Maoism. Therefore how to create a systematical theory to guide the future development of China, either traditional socialism or Chinese socialism is crucial and challenging.

8.2 ENTITLEMENT

In a world, where there will be no dominating power and each major power has the nuclear capacity, the world entitlement does not actually exist, simply no major world power would like to risk herself to defend a remotely small kingdom such as Taiwan, where people happily conduct the small-kingdom life. Also there would be little ideological difference between major world powers, if there would be no breakthrough in systematical thoughts on distribution of social wealth and exercise of social justice.

So the world entitlement will downgrade to the regional entitlement, although the US would still assume her world entitlement with too many out-of-date treaties. With the less and less role played by the US, the historical trend would suggest that the US might tend towards her traditional isolationism in pan-America, where the resources are still rich, but then it would be the ending point of WTO, because the isolationism would lead to the protectionism.

The EU actually has little entitlement to assume because their economy is more likely to be conducted within EU, and their interests are limited mainly in EU.

Japan as her market and resource are all located outside, so Japan may have more regional entitlement as the US is phasing out from this world, especially in Asia because the history shows that the Japanese active zone was generally limited to Asia. Still the history shows that Japan has attacked Russia in 1904 and

US in 1941 without declaration of war because her thought is different from those in continental countries when Japan was in desperate situation. Thus Japan could attack North Korea as her maximal entitlement in this region.

Russia would assume her traditional entitlement, however if Russia could not find a systematical thought to support her entitlement worldwide, her role would be limited to her surrounding countries as we have seen how difficulty the wars were conducted in Afghanistan and Chechnya recently.

Perhaps, as China more and more depends on world resources and world market, and as the Chinese industry continues developing, the Chinese could change from an internal-oriented national to an external-oriented national through decades. In that case, the Chinese would have some limited entitlements. However, this entitlement would be more likely to direct to Africa and Middle East where China gets raw materials.

A purely economic power could be a way that the Chinese hope to become a world power, because the Chinese economy grows still very fast. However, the Lanchester's laws suggest that China still has a long way to go to lead the trend in world economy.

The history has already shown how the world powers obtained their world entitlements, the UK needed to sell her goods around world in 18th and 19th centuries, the Soviet Union needed to let the Marxism-Leninism spread around world after World War II, the Japan needed to control Asia during World War II, etc. So what would China need?

On their way to assume the world power, the history leaves some clues such as Lord Palmerston said [64]: "Nations have no permanent friends or allies, they only have permanent interests", and Japan desperately attacked the world without any hope of success in World War II.

I would suggest that the Chinese are not special in world entitlement, not only because of the reasons discussed in previous chapters, but also because the Chinese are too naïve in international affairs as shown by history.

8.3 Opportunity

The opportunity, itself, is an event with small probability, especially the event with great impact [40], but the event with small probability is very hard to predict.

Honestly and frankly speaking, the Chinese are good at catching the small opportunities although the importance of an opportunity is viewed differently from person to person. Besides, the Chinese proverb, "tian shi, di li, ren he" (see section 2.2.3 Opportunity), several other Chinese proverbs can demonstrate that

Table 1 (Continued)

Fable	Moral explained by Non-Chinese	Moral explained by Chinese	Note
The Cat And The Birds	A villain may disguise himself, but he will not deceive the wise.	Even villains pretend very kind, a wise knows that they are the people honey-mouthed and dagger-hearted.	Same or similar
The Spendthrift and the Swallow	One swallow does not make summer.	It is dangerous if you do not follow nature law.	Not same or similar
The Old Woman and the Doctor	There are few good offices done for other people, which the benefactor does not hope to be the better for himself [75].	The extremely greedy person always unconsciously leaves his guilt evidence.	Undecided
The Moon and her Mother	Someone who is always changing cannot expect others to regard him as one particular thing [72].	Things always change, cannot be done once forever.	Undecided
Mercury and the Woodman	Honesty is the best policy.	The honest people get help from others, the guile people are spurned by others.	Same or similar
The Ass, The Fox, and The Lion	Betray a friend, and you'll often find you have ruined yourself.	The person, who betrays friend and friendship, will not have a good end.	Same or similar
The Lion And The Mouse	Little friends may prove great friends. No act of kindness, no matter how small, is ever wasted [76].	Luck changes in turn, and there is the time that the strong needs the weak.	Undecided
The Crow And The Pitcher	Necessity is the mother of invention.	Wisdom can win strength.	Not same or similar
The Boys and The Frogs	What we do in sport often makes great trouble for others [73].	Do not build one's happiness on other's suffering.	Same or similar
The North Wind and The Sun	Persuasion is better than force.	Persuasion is better than force.	Same or similar

Fable	**Moral explained by Non-Chinese**	**Moral explained by Chinese**	**Note**
The Mistress and Her Servants		Many people's unluck is made by themselves.	No comparison
The Goods and The Ills		It is not easy for people to meet goods, but people are hurt every day by ills.	No comparison
The Hares and The Frogs	There is always someone worse off than yourself [77].	The unfortunate people often comfort themselves by the fact that some people are more unfortunate.	Undecided
The Fox and The Stork	One bad turn deserves another.	If you want others to respect to you, you should at first respect others. Meanwhile, the best way to treat the people who do not respect others is to use their approaches to treat them.	Same or similar
The Wolf in Sheep's Clothing	Appearances are deceptive [78].	Sometimes the appearance hides the essence, so we cannot make the judgment based only on appearance.	Same or similar
The Stag in the Ox-Stall	What is safety to one is not always safety to another [74].	Do not ignore other danger when running away from a danger.	Not same or similar
The Milkmaid and Her Pail	Do not count your chickens before they are hatched.	To think impossible will not bring any real benefit.	Same or similar
The Dolphins, The Whales, and The Sprat	Those who get too caught up in what they're doing lose all sense of perspective [78].	Some people are actually not important at all, but they will consider themselves hero during trouble time.	Not same or similar
The Fox and The Monkey	Boasters brag most when they cannot be detected.	Without other people's rebut, the liar will boast himself more.	Same or similar

Table 1 (Continued)

Fable	Moral explained by Non-Chinese	Moral explained by Chinese	Note
The Ass and The Lap-Dog	Clumsy jesting is no joke [75].	The same thing may not be suitable for all the people.	Not same or similar
The Fir-Tree and The Bramble	Better poverty without a care than wealth with its many obligations.	The unromantic life may be less pain and dangerous than the fantastic-rich life.	Same or similar
The Frogs' Complaint Against The Sun	Watch the actions of your enemy [75].	Many people lacking of thought can only follow others to make a row.	Not same or similar
The Dog, The Cock, and The Fox	Those who try to entrap others are sometimes caught by their own schemes [73].	The wise people would not fall chaos when facing danger and can easily and cleverly defeat enemy.	Undecided
The Gnat and The Bull	We may often be of more consequence in our own eyes than in the eyes of our neighbors.	For these, who are weak and unknowledgeable, other people would not feel their existence important.	Not same or similar
The Bear and The Travelers	Misfortune tests the sincerity of friendship	The people, who cannot face difficulty together, are not real friends.	Same or similar
The Slave and The Lion	Return favors and favors will be bestowed on you [75].	The people, who do goodness, will get goodness.	Same or similar
The Flea and The Man	Do not waste your pity on a scamp.	It is absolute to punish the bad people no matter if they are small or large.	Undecided
The Bee and Jupiter	Evil wishes, like fowls, come home to roost.	The people, who do not have good willing, but get bad results themselves.	Undecided
The Oak and The Reeds	Stoop to conquer [74].	It could be better for oneself sometimes if he is not unwisely against the people, who are stronger than him.	Undecided

Fable	**Moral explained by Non-Chinese**	**Moral explained by Chinese**	**Note**
The Blind Man and The Cub	Evil tendencies are early shown.	Evil habit can be known at childhood.	Same or similar
The Boy and The Snails	Nothing can be well that's out of season [75].	People often blame those, who do not distinguish the situations.	Undecided
The Apes and The Two Travelers	Don't always assume the values of others match your own [78].	Many people prefer to believe in flattered lies, but do not like to listen to truth.	Not same or similar
The Ass and His Burdens	You may play a good card once too often	Some wise people fail due to their wise, so they hurt themselves.	Same or similar
The Shepherd's Boy and the Wolf	You cannot believe a liar even when he tells the truth	Those, who often tell lies, cannot be believed in when they tell the truth.	Same or similar
The Fox and The Goat	Look before your leap.	The wise should clearly consider the results before doing something, and then do it.	Same or similar
The Fisherman and The Sprat	A fish in the hand is worth two in the sea [72].	It is only the foolish people, who give up a small benefit in hand, but pursue the illusory big benefit.	Same or similar
The Boasting Traveler	Deeds, not words.	For the fact, which is easily proved by other fact, the more speech would be redundant.	Same or similar
The Crab and His Mother	Example is better than precept.	The educator should himself conduct an honest life, and go along an honest way, and then he can teach others.	Not same or similar

S

Y